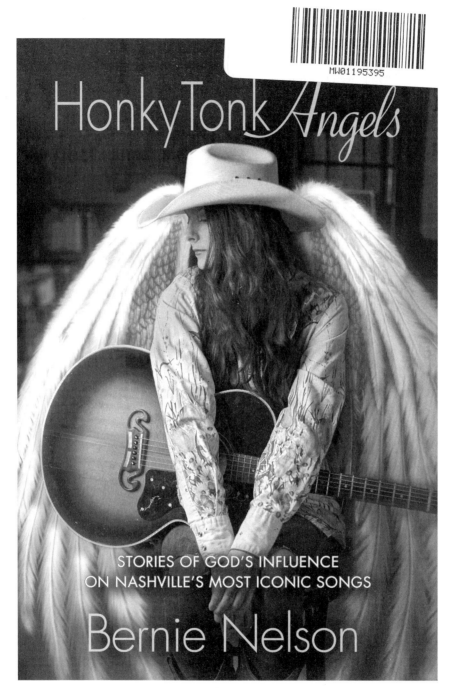

HonkyTonk *Angels*

STORIES OF GOD'S INFLUENCE
ON NASHVILLE'S MOST ICONIC SONGS

Bernie Nelson

HERITAGE BUILDERS
PUBLISHING

Honky Tonk Angels

Bernie Nelson

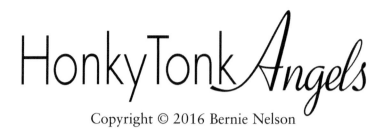

HonkyTonk Angels

Published by Heritage Builders Publishing
Monterey California

Credits

Cover photograph by: Wes Bowker
Cover model: Star Hanner
Boots courtesy of: French's Boots
The Wanted Saloon Dickson Tennessee
Back Cover photograph by: Lou Chantry
Back Cover model : Kimber Annie Engstrom
Songwriter Sketches: Jeanne Petersen
Bart Herbison Executive Director at the NSAI for story contributions
Bernie also wishes to thank David Hall, and his pal Even Stevens for the introduction to Heritage Builders Publishing, and Diamond Gusset Jeans and Kay Ellis for their support.
Karon Hetherington and Pam Lewis Proof readers
Dr Sherm Smith, Publisher and Editor Dr Lee Fredrickson

ISBN: 978-1-94260360-3

Visit our website at: www.heritagebuilderspublishing.com
Printed in the United States of America

HERITAGE BUILDERS
PUBLISHING

ACKNOWLEDGMENTS

Bernie would like to thank those incredibly generous giants who took the time to share their wisdom and talents over the years. Without them he would have loaded up his car and went back to Colorado long before his journey even began. So he would like to say thank you to them, in chronological order:

Robert Byrne
Mac McAnally
Barry Beckett
Jerry Crutchfield
Bob Montgomery
Peter Svenson
Jim Malloy
Thom Schuyler
Don Schlitz
Dave Loggins
Russell Smith
J.T. Martin
Lisa Silvers
Mike Robertson
Norro Wilson
Mentor Williams
Steve Cropper
Buck Moore
Fred Foster
Larry Jon Wilson
Joe Gilchrist
Red Lane
Wayne Carson
Jeff Hanna
Jimmy Fadden

Guy Clark
Duane Eddy
Chris LeDoux
Vince Gill
John Prine
Bob Doyle
Harold Shedd
Amy Kurland
Mervin Lougue
Richard Leigh
Wayland Holyfield
Rick Blackburn
Rick Hall
Martha Sharp
Mary Martin
Tony Brown
Charlie Monk
Blake Mevis
David Preston
Celia Frolieg
Even Stevens
Dennis Morgan
George McCorkle
Kevin Lamb

CONTENTS

My first cut...

February 10, 1987

Ain't No Binds

The Whites

"I'd rather be alone tonight,
than lonely there with you."

PREFACE

I would say that when I first came to Nashville my level of spirituality was at best muddied under my raw enthusiasm to find my place in this spinning, rapidly door-opening world of songwriting and the country music scene as a whole.

Don't get me wrong with every door that did open; I was always thankful. But I credit that to my Catholic upbringing. I wasn't aware of the power of faith and thankfulness at that early part of my career. To have faith and thankfulness in something yet unseen, would not be a part of my daily world 'til long after I had seen my first few cuts. Nor did I see the connection to obvious divine intervention 'til after my first successes as well.

In looking back at my victories and shortcomings, I remember back to before I got my first cut. I asked veteran hit songwriter Dave Loggins what I was doing wrong. After he pointed out my unpolished lyrics and need for stronger melodies and showed me where to find them, he gave me my most important advice ever. He compared getting a cut to the first time you hit a baseball just right for a home run. Up until that moment, you can't grasp how it feels. Once you do, though, you know that feeling, and you never doubt it again. He told me to imagine that I already had the cuts, and that they were coming faster and faster, and that I should convince myself not that they would happen, but they had already taken place. It worked of course, and the cuts came quickly after that. Years later, I was reading the many miracles of Christ and noticed that one thing stuck out to me that happened right before each miracle. Before turning the water into wine, the feeding of the multitudes, and the raising of Lazarus from the dead, He always thanked God for the miracles before they happened. Jesus wasn't thanking God for something that was about to happen but for something that in his mind had already taken place. Wow. Talent added to faith, combined with patience in God's plan, will always equate to success.

I have met my share of angels in my life. I also believe that God has used me in the role of an Earthly angel. Now, I'm no saint—ask my mom—but I have no doubt that He has put me in places to make certain things in my life and other's lives happen to His good. One day a few years back, I saw a man walking down the road by my house. I noticed that he was limping and carrying a pillowcase filled with what I assumed were his entire belongings. I was running late for an appointment in Nashville 40 minutes away but turned around to see if the man needed a ride. When I got alongside of him, I asked where he was going, and with the most peaceful face he said, "I'm not sure, but I will know it when I get there."

I asked if he needed a ride. He told me he was fine, and that God had him right where he needed to be. I asked if he needed money or water. Again with a smile and peacefulness that stirred me, he said, "I have everything I need but thank you."

I drove away totally confused. Why did God want me to help him if he wouldn't take a ride or money from me? I wasn't there for him; he was there for me. Angels are here right now while I write this book. They have whispered words to me that I would never have chosen otherwise, and they brought this book to life in so many amazing ways. These stories represent pieces of a lot of people's lives. Please look at them not as stories on paper but as windows into the souls of some of the most amazing poets and storytellers of our time. I don't know why God allowed me to be a songwriter, but I know this—we all have gifts, and the gifts are meant to be used for His good. I would like to also say that for those struggling with doubt and possibly rejection, angels are real and God's timing is perfect. Music is the language of angels.

—Bernie Nelson

Bernie working hard on another chapter in Honky Tonk Angels 2016

Old Flame

There's an old flame
burning in your eyes, that
tears can't drown and make
up can't disguise.

Chapter 1

Mac McAnally

Donny Lowery

OLD FLAME...ALABAMA

My first day in Nashville was probably much the same as most people that pack up everything they own in a POS car and drive across the country for two days with $642 in their pocket to a place they know nothing about. I was excited, anxious, tired, eager, but most of all terrified at the prospect of total failure.

I could get the band back together in Colorado. I could tell them that the timing wasn't right, that Nashville was going through a crazy pop faze, that my kind of songs weren't popular right now. Heck, they didn't want me to leave in the first place.

It was October 26, 1984, and I knew very few people in Nashville. Jerry Crutchfield, produced hits on Lee Greenwood,

"Do not forget to show hospitality to strangers, for by doing, some people have shown hospitality to angels without even knowing it."
Hebrews 13:2

Tanya Tucker, and the Oak Ridge Boys, had given me a single song contract offer at MCA Music. The song-pluggers there had already placed a song of mine on hold, meaning that the artist or record label was considering recording the song, with Conway Twitty. That surely had to count for something. This whole getting songs on radio thing shouldn't take any time at all. Yeah, right!

A year earlier, I had been down in Muscle Shoals, Alabama recording with a couple of songwriter/producers that already had me rethinking the whole, "I'm gonna be a songwriter/artist/superstar idea."

Mac McAnally. "Back Where I Come From" for Kenny Chesney was a tall, country bumpkin looking redheaded, and a multi-talented songwriting fool.

He and Robert Byrne, "That Was a Close One," Earl Thomas Conley, had heard a few songs of mine from a friend that went to school with Robert. Both of these guys were beyond impressive back then. They both would go on to be two of the biggest writer/producers of the 80's, and 90's in country music.

One night while I was staying with Mac at his house in Muscle Shoals, we were sitting around waiting for Alan Schulman, one of the studio engineers at Wishbone Music in Muscle Shoals, to return with a bottle of bootleg Jack Daniels. My luggage was accidentally sent to Tupelo, Mississippi with my bottle of Jack in it, and Muscle Shoals was a dry county back then.

I knew little about Mac at that point but was already sensing his presence and respect in Muscle Shoals and the rest of the music world. He had been opening for James Taylor and was signed to RCA with a pop record out and charting a single as well. His voice was southern country with a unique gentleness about it, and some guy named Jimmy Buffett had just cut his song "It's My Job." Cha-ching!

While we were sitting there, Mac sat down at his white Yamaha baby grand piano and said,

"Hey, you're country, I want to get your opinion on a song Donny Lowery and I are working on."

Three minutes later, I was feeling like the kid that just got a peek behind the curtain of the Great and All Knowing Oz. Mac played me what would go on to become one of Alabama's biggest singles, "Old Flame." It knocked me out, but made me sadly aware of my place in the pecking order of creativity and overall talent.

Mac said that Ronnie Milsap had it on hold, but that some new act that just got signed to RCA wanted it... ALABAMA. I told him,

"Man you gotta get Milsap to record that. It would be huge!"

As we all know, ALABAMA did go on to record it, and I watched it go up, up, up the charts until it went to #1.

That was my first insight into "Honky Tonk Angels," those clever wisps of grace that show up and miraculously get the song to just the right person at just the right time.

There is one thing that I am certain of in my lengthy journey in this up and down, unpredictable world we call country music. Without God's amazing timing and kindness, the biggest songs that played on country radio never would have had a snowball's chance in.....well, you know.

On the Other Hand

On the other hand is a golden band, to remind me of the one who would not understand.

Chapter 2

Don Shutz

Paul Overstreet

ON THE OTHER HAND

Like I said, Jerry Crutchfield was running MCA Music at the time and for whatever reason, I'll never know, said he liked what I was doing and wanted me to hang around and turn songs in for consideration. MCA was a small building on 17th Avenue South. There were just a few writers signed there but man, that place was about to blow the roof off the other big publishers just down the street.

My first day there I walked right into Dave Loggins. I knew Dave from his huge pop hit, "Please Come To Boston," but I had also been a fan of his other songs that he recorded on a record called *One Way Ticket to Paradise*. Are you kidding me,

Dave Loggins writes here? How dang cool is that? I also met a guy wearing orange corduroy pants and a ratty looking t-shirt with a big ol' head of hair. I thought, "Man I know him, that's Don Schlitz, he wrote "The Gambler!" Don was puffing on a cigarette that he had bummed from Loggins. (Something I later found out was that Schlitz never bought his own cigarettes. Neither did Loggins, it seemed.)

Neither Don nor Dave had done much co-writing prior to MCA but would collaborate on several mega hits very soon.

A few days later, I met Russell Smith from The Amazing Rhythm Aces, "Third Rate Romance." He said "hi." We talked, and he was kind enough to listen to a few of my songs. I knew early on that this place was like Camelot, the center of the known country universe, and I was smack dab in the middle of it. The problem was the only thing I could write was a bad check.

Russell Smith and I got together soon after and started co-writing. Bobby Bare recorded our first song, "When To Give Up," but the album never saw daylight.

One day, we were writing in Loggins writing room at the end of the hall. MCA had three writing rooms in it back then directly across from the tape/gathering/smoking/patting each other on the back room.

Schlitz was in the middle room with Paul Overstreet, "Deeper Than The Holler," and "When You Say Nothing At All." I had seen Paul play at the Bluebird Café, and really liked his hardcore country voice and songs.

The walls were paper-thin between those three writing rooms, and you could really hear the other writers when they would get into what they were working on. That day, Don and Paul were playing with a stone country melody and really clever hook. It was so cornball country that when we all merged in the tape room before lunch, Russell and Don were singing harmony and joking about how country the song was, and trying to figure out who would possibly record such a dinosaur. At the time, "Restless Heart" was taking off and crossing into the pop market. Lee Greenwood was cranking out "poppier" songs and a whole lot of other acts were headed in that direction. The song Don Schlitz and Paul Overstreet were writing that day was called "On The Other Hand."

Randy Bruce Traywick moved to Nashville in the early 80's and started working at the Nashville Palace out on McGavock Pike across from the Opryland Hotel as a part-time singer and full-time cook.

Some time after he changed his name to Randy Travis, he recorded his first album for Warner Bros.

Pat Higdon was a song plugger at MCA Music at the time and knew that "On the Other Hand" was a really good song, but that it had a limited amount of places he could run with it. Martha Sharp at Warner Brothers Records was one of those places.

Storms of Life was Randy's first album. The record label knew that testing the radio waters with an extremely traditional country song would be risky, but they went ahead and put "On the Other Hand" out to radio as Randy Travis' first single. A lot of people today don't know that it fared miserably.

Never even breaking into the Top 40, it appeared that the clever-hooked, stone country song that Don Schlitz and Paul Overstreet wrote one day in the not-too-soundproof writing rooms at MCA Music was headed to Country Radio purgatory.

After Randy's first two efforts to radio failed, Warner Bros decided to release a song called "1982."

Ding, ding, ding, ding, we have a winner! That song wouldn't slow down until it went to #2.

But while Warner Brothers marketing and promotion staff were high-fiving each other about their new-found money maker, (*Storms of Life* would sell over 4 million records), they were facing the question of what the heck do we have left on the record to follow this hit "1982" with?

Enter the "Honky Tonk Angels." As fate (God) would have it, there really wasn't another single on the Storms of Life record. The bullpen was empty; time to go to Plan B. Lib Hatcher, Randy's manager and later-to-be wife, was insistent on re-releasing "On The Other Hand." Crazy, no one does that. Well, sometimes crazy goes a long way. "On the Other Hand" was Randy Travis' first #1 single. Proof that God is ever so happy to help out sometimes. Psalms 103:20.

The Dance

I could've missed the pain, but
I'd a had to miss the dance.

Chapter 3

TONY ARATA

Tony Arata

THE DANCE

I had my first cut on The Whites on MCA Records in 1986 and started getting other cuts shortly after that with Neal McCoy and John Anderson among others. My first writing deal was the result of my pal Roger Brown, "We Must Be Loving Right," George Strait, and Micki Foster insisting that I go see Norro Wilson at Merit Music. Roger and I had written a few really good songs and Micki, well heck, she was music row royalty. She was the daughter of Fred Foster the man that basically invented the vocal booth, Roy Orbison and Kris Kristofferson. Merit Music was another lightly staffed publishing company but was also packed with some legendary hitters like Steve Cropper "Sitting On the Dock of The Bay," "Knock On Wood," a member of the Blues Brothers, Booker T and the MG's, Buck Moore

23

Bernie with Garth Brooks
Songwriter Hall of Fame
dinner 2011

"The Box" and "Paint Me a Birmingham," and Mentor Williams "Drift Away."

Norro Wilson was no slouch himself. He discovered John Anderson, John Conlee, and wrote, oh yeah, "The Grand Tour" George Jones, 1974.

I signed with Merit Music, April of 1986. Having a writing deal helped me out financially, so when Roger Brown said that he had found a cool house not far from Music Row for rent for only six hundred dollars, I jumped. It was a big sucker with a back yard, and I got the master bedroom by way of a lottery that I cheated on.... Sorry Roger.

I was playing regularly at Douglas Corner Café, which was closer to the house and a little funkier then The Bluebird Café. I was in great company with Roger Brown, Jimmy Stewart, "Little Less Talk" for Toby Keith, "Brotherly Love" on Keith Whitley, Tony Arata, "Thank You I'm Holding My Own" for Lee Roy Parnell, and "The Dance" for Garth Brooks. It reminded me of some of the bars where I played with my band in Wyoming and South Dakota; old brick, long, and full of character. Back then the sound systems left a lot to be desired, but we had a good time just the same.

One Saturday morning, while I was sleeping in the master bedroom in the big house not far from Music Row, Roger Brown knocked on my door to tell me that there was an ad in the paper for exotic cowboy boots for one hundred dollars. "No way," I said. So Roger produced an ad showing me ostrich boots for one hundred dollars. I had a Jeep CJ7. Roger and I headed north on I-65 with the top off to find this place that had the great deal on cowboy boots. Now, back in those days, the only things songwriters spent money on were new pickup trucks and cowboy boots. So this could potentially be a huge score. Neither one of us had one hundred dollars, but we figured what the heck else we got to do on a Saturday in Twangtown.

Cowtown Boots was right off Gallatin Pike just north of the Rivergate Mall. As soon as I walked in, I saw the best pair of boots I'd ever seen. They were peanut brittle colored and if that wasn't enough, they were a size 10.

I was trying them on, and thinking to myself that I could just not eat for the rest of the month and maybe that would help me justify buying the boots when a voice from behind me said,

"Hey, are you Bernie Nelson?"

The voice was coming from a young salesman wearing a gray colored cowboy hat, striped shirt, Wranglers, and looking like he just stepped off the cover of *Western Horseman* magazine.

I said, "Yeah."

"Cool," he said, "I'm Garth Brooks."

I'd heard of Garth because my former ASCAP Rep, Bob Doyle and his business partner, Pam Lewis, were managing him.

After persuading the young Mr. Brooks to hold my hot check for a few days, Roger and I walked out of Cowtown Boots the proud owners of two brand new pairs of smokin boots. Before we left, though, we asked Garth to come to Douglas Corner and sit in with us and play sometime, which he would soon do.

I first met Tony Arata in 1984 at the Country Radio Seminar, which back then was held at the Opryland Hotel. I will always remember it as being the first time I was elbow to elbow with the biggest stars in country music. Most of the gatherings were in massive ballrooms where the artist would walk around and talk to radio personalities to promote their new single. It was only my first year in Nashville, so I was the wide-eyed kid still wearing the cowboy hat I came to town in.

Tony had a song he had written on radio with Jim Glasier called, "The Man In The Mirror." Right away, I was drawn to Tony's unusual lyrics and style as a songwriter.

Tony and his wife, Jami, moved to Nashville the following year, and he was writing for Noble Vision, which was under the umbrella of hit-maker Dennis Morgan on 18th Avenue.

My roommate, Roger Brown, and Tony would start writing and doing songwriter nights together which would eventually put Tony Arata and me together on the same stage very early on at the Douglas Corner Cafe.

I don't remember exactly what night it was that Garth first joined us at Douglas Corner, but I do remember the round. It was Tony Arata, me, Jimmy Stewart, and Kevin Welch, "Til I'm Too Old To Die Young," Moe Bandy.

We got Garth up and after a few go-arounds Tony said, "Well here's a brand new song," and proceeded to introduce me, Jimmy, Kevin Welch, and everyone else that was there that night to a powerful song about love and life and how, if it is the right one, it is worth all that it costs. A song called "The Dance." It's hard to explain what it was like hearing it for the first time, but I remember thinking that it was a very heavy song. Garth had heard Tony play the song in a round at the Bluebird Cafe a few weeks earlier and reminded Tony, "If I ever get the chance, I want to record that song." At the time, that seemed like a pretty long shot for both the song and the singer.

The melody for the song had been in Tony's pocket for awhile but with a different set of lyrics. Do you know that Honky Tonk Angels love a good movie?

Tony Arata and his wife, Jami, had gone to the movies to see *Peggy Sue Got Married* starring Kathleen Turner. Tony tells of the part in the movie where Peggy Sue gets to go back in time, and not marry her high school sweetheart because she now knows how it will all end up. When she returns to the present, the locket that she was wearing with her children from that marriage disappeared because they would never have happened.

Tony sat down with his old favorite melody and re-wrote every word in "The Dance."

He told me that she had realized that the pain she had suffered in the marriage was worth the gift of her children and had she not "danced' with her now ex-husband years ago, none of that would have happened. Wow!

Every label had turned down Doyle/Lewis and their artist, Garth Brooks. Finally, after an arranged showcase at the Bluebird, Capitol Record's Lynn Shultz got to hear a new song of Garth's, "If Tomorrow Never Comes," which he had just written with Kent Blazy. Mr. Shultz told Bob Doyle that he would like to talk to them about a possible deal. Garth ended up with a one-shot record deal on Capitol Records.

Allen Reynolds cut an extremely haunting track with Garth on "The Dance." A lot of reverb made his vocal all the more haunting, and the piano played that day by Bobby Woods was amazing. Dang, could it have sounded any bigger?

Garth Brooks by the following summer, after the release of his debut record, had already recorded all the songs for the next album *No Fences*, and the lead-off single that summer was slated to be "Friends In Low Places," but producer Allen Reynolds had a gnawing feeling about "The Dance." He persuaded the record label head, Jimmy Bowen, to go to a concert of Garth's and see the response to the song.

The song, the performance, the video, so many things were so perfect. There's no way that anyone could have orchestrated the results of the song; no one except God and His little angels that from day one fell in love with "The Dance."

I Can't Make
You Love Me

Turn down the lights, turn
down the bed. Turn down
these voices inside my head.

CHAPTER 4

Allen Shamblin

Mike Reid

"I CAN'T MAKE YOU."...A BLUEGRASS SONG

What would the chances be for a former two-time Pro Bowl NFL tackle and an Austin, Texas house appraiser getting together in Nashville, Tennessee to write one of the all time greatest lost love songs ever recorded? Well, if you have Honky Tonk Angels hanging all around your world, pretty darn good.

Mike Reid played football at Penn State and was team captain for both seasons that they went undefeated, '68 and '69.

He then played five seasons with the Cincinnati Bengals and earned two trips to the postseason Pro Bowl in '72 and '73. Not

"Come near to God and HE will come near to you."
James 4-8

exactly the background you would find for most country songwriters that end up in the Nashville Songwriters Association International Hall of Fame.

After graduating from Sam Houston University, Allen Shamblin worked as a real estate appraiser in Austin, Texas. In 1987, Allen moved to Nashville to be a songwriter much to his father's dismay. Allen had felt that he was headed in the wrong direction with his life in Austin, so one night he asked God,

"What do you want me to do?"

God responded to Allen by saying, " What do you want to do?"

It didn't take him long to decide.

He said, "Write songs," so write songs it would be.

Allen Shamblin came into my radar by way of Dave Gibson, "Ships That Don't Come In," "Queen of Memphis," "Lonely and Gone." Dave told me that I should write with him, so Allen and I set a date to write and he came over to my two bedroom duplex one block off of Belmont Blvd. It would be our first of over thirty songs or more written together including multi-platinum cuts on Kenny Chesney, Wynonna, and Ricky Van Shelton.

Just a side note—One day in that same two-bedroom brick duplex, Allen would show up for a co-write with a tall drink of water cowboy looking fella named Chris LeDoux.

Mike Reid and Allen Shamblin had been working on a Bluegrass feeling up-tempo song called "I Can't Make You Love Me." In an early morning co-write, that would be their sixth time to fix and finish this song, Allen walked into the room where Mike was sitting at his piano; the same piano where the two of them had written so many great songs before. They had written many for Mike's career as an artist, including the rebel rousing hit "Walk On Faith." The night before, those all too often passion filled Honky Tonk Angels had visited Mike in the way of a piece of music that would forever go on to be so easily recognized.

What had been an up-tempo Bluegrass song would soon be transformed into one of the American pop world's greatest and most recorded songs.

When Allen heard the melody of the opening verses, he told Mike it was such a great melody that he should never put words to it because it was so haunting.

Mike smiled and proceeded to sing, "Turn down the lights, turn down the bed. Turn down these voices inside my head...." "I Can't Make You Love Me." Thanks God for reminding us that You can't make us love You but that You will always love us.

A Boy
Named Sue

I grew up quick and I grew up mean. My fists got hard and my wits got keen. I roamed from town to town to hide my shame...

Chapter 5

SHEL SILVERSTIEN

Shel Silverstein

A BOY NAMED SUE

Oh, to have been a fly on the wall or an angel the night that Johnny Cash had a few friends over to his house in Hendersonville, Tennessee, February 1969. A true treasure chest of who's who came to visit and be a part of what would become one of the most amazing "guitar pulls" of all time. That night, his guests would take turns with the guitar and pull out some of their most recent hits and eventually their new songs.

Throughout the course of the evening, John and June would hear and be introduced to classics for the first time as Bob Dylan sang "Lay Lady Lay." Joni Mitchell sang "Both Sides Now," Kris Kristofferson did "Me And Bobby McGee," Graham Nash sang "Marrakesh Express," and a hilarious satire about a man

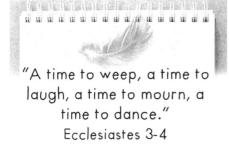

"A time to weep, a time to laugh, a time to mourn, a time to dance."

Ecclesiastes 3-4

whose father was not going to be around to help his son grow up, and so he gave his son a feminine name. That song would be a tune written by Shel Silverstein called, "A Boy Named Sue."

To say that Shel Silverstein was a songwriter is like saying Moses was a travel guide.

Born September 25, 1930, in Chicago, Illinois, Shel would try his hand at success with his cartoons early on at the two universities he attended, The University of Illinois, which he would be expelled from, and the Chicago Academy of Fine Arts. While at the Chicago Academy of Fine Arts, he was drafted into the army and had his earliest cartoons placed in *Pacific Stars and Stripes* magazine. After his stint with Uncle Sam, he returned to Chicago where he soon had placements with his cartoons in *Look, Sports Illustrated,* and *This Week* magazines. His biggest break as a cartoonist would come from *Playboy* magazine in 1957 where he would become famous for his satirical cartoons over a twenty-year period. But drawing cartoons was only one of Shel's gifts to the world. He would go on to author many children's books including the still popular *The Giving Tree.*

Songwriting seemed to flow out of Shel in those days and after collaborations with Chicago's own Steve Goodman, "You Never Even Called Me By My Name," he soon found his way, like so many others, to the streets of Nashville.

As a songwriter, Silverstein would find his place on the country music charts with songs like "Put Another Log On the Fire" for Tompall Glaser, and Loretta Lynn's "One's On The Way." He also had a slew of hits for the rowdy pop/country group, Dr. Hook; songs like, "Sylvia's Mother" and the landmark, "Cover Of The Rolling Stone."

Silverstein had made friends with the Cash's and was fortunately at Johnny's house that fateful night that pop and country icons gathered to twang out their latest hits-to-be.

So there was "A Boy Named Sue" being played for everyone at the party. Johnny loved it and told Silverstein that he would like a copy of the lyrics. He was headed to California the very next day to record a follow-up recording at San Quentin prison. June told Johnny that he should play the song for the inmates and see if it worked for the new record. Johnny told her that he didn't have time to learn the song but would take the lyrics with him just the same. June could be very persuasive when it came to song selection for her husband in those days. Now we all know that God is ever so present in prison, so it should come as no surprise that his Honky Tonk Angels would tag along just in case there was any work that needed to be done.

I think, as a songwriter and artist, you always know that you have to try out new songs somewhere eventually, so Mr. Cash felt that if he didn't get the lyrics right at the San Quentin show, he would polish them up afterward. He was feeling for some reason the need to play the song that night. When you hear the live record of the song you can hear in a couple places where Johnny stepped out of the pocket and didn't exactly follow the band when they changed chords a few times. Despite the lack of perfection on the delivery, Johnny found himself getting caught up in the inmates' response to a song about a boy whose father left him at an early age; a song about growing up getting into fights all the time and getting picked on. Hmmm, wonder what made June think that a song like that would go over in prison?

He was so unfamiliar with the lyrics that he taped them to a music stand the night of the show and was reading them as he sang the song for the second time. He had only sung the song one other time, which was the night before but when he felt the crowd of prisoners cheering along and getting caught up in the song, he really started to put the Johnny Cash stamp on the performance. The sound of him shouting, "My name is Sue, How do you do, Now you're gonna die!" will be forever embedded into the country music landscape.

Both Johnny Cash and Shel Silverstein are now gone, but it leaves me to wonder: What was it that made Shel go to Johnny's house that night? Why did June insist that her husband take the song with him to play live when she knew how important the recording would be? And finally, what was it that made Johnny Cash step out of his planned set list and introduce a song so new that he was barely able to perform it without reading the lyrics?

I guess we will never really know, but my thoughts tend to sway towards those angels that knew that inmates locked up in prison have a need to connect with something, someone that resonates with their former selves. I believe Honky Tonk Angels got a visitor's pass that day and were there the day that "A Boy Named Sue" came to be.

Delta Dawn

And did I hear you say he was meeting you here today, to take you to his mansion in the sky...

Chapter 6

Alex Harvey

DELTA DAWN

Nashville is intertwined in so many ways. Dottie West, "Country Sunshine," was performing at the Palomino in LA, so a bunch of songwriters and band members decided to go catch her show one night.

It was 1973, and in the crowd were members of Buck Owens' band, Merle Haggard's band, and Glen Campbell's bass player. Also hanging out were two fairly new songwriters, Larry Collins and Alex Harvey. Larry

Larry Collins

In My Father's house
are many rooms. If it
were not so, would I
have told you that I am
going there to prepare
a place for you? And if I
go and prepare a place
for you, I will come back
and welcome you into
My presence, so that you
also may be where I am....
John 14:2-3

and Alex were fresh off a hit song called, "Tulsa Turn-around," which had been recorded by Sammy Davis Jr. and Three Dog Night as well.

After what I can only imagine were a few adult beverages consumed, the group of twang interpreters headed to Larry Collins' house for more picking and drinking.

Sometime around 3 am, most of the guys were sleeping with only Larry and Alex Harvey still sitting up with guitars. What a great time to introduce God into all of this. It's not as if He was ever absent from the gathering, but it was at that moment that He put His angels to work to inspire what would become one of the greatest country songs ever recorded.

In 1963, Alex Harvey was 15 years old and living just outside of Memphis, Tennessee when his band won a contest that he was certain was his ticket out of Blues Town, USA. His mother told him she wanted to go with him to see him perform at the show. Alex Harvey had reasons not to want his mother to go with him or even be there. She had been known to drink and get out of control. This was a big deal to Alex, and he didn't want his mother showing up intoxicated and ruining any chance that might come out of this big break, so he told her that he didn't want her to go because she would embarrass him.

Alex and his band taped the show in Jackson, and then made the 90-mile drive back to West Tennessee. When he got home, his mother was nowhere to be found. He was sitting around the house when about dusk, a black Buick rolled up the hill, and two ladies he knew got out. They said to him,

"Your momma is gone."

He asked them gone where, and they explained that she had died. They told him that she had driven her car into a tree at a high rate of speed.

For years, he blamed himself for her death. A young man with guilt and motherless had two choices; get into drugs and alcohol, or put your feelings into your music. Alex Harvey made somewhat of a compromise, and his songs have shown the depth of his inspiration that has separated him from the other artist-writers of his time for that very reason.

Okay, lets go back to that guitar jam at Larry Collins' house with two new writers and a bunch of road warriors laying around after a Dottie West show at the LA Palomino.

God uses what we call mistakes and misfortunes all the time. He usually puts a little distance between us and those mistakes before they manifest themselves to us. But have no doubt, God is fully aware of what He is doing, and how it will impact you in time.

What gift could God possibly give Alex Harvey to replace the guilt he carried over all those years? Alex will tell you that while he was sitting there at Larry's house, he saw his mother sitting in a rocking chair across the room from him. He remembered and thought it was odd that his mother's father always called her "Baby," even though she was over forty years old. She was also raised in the Mississippi Delta and was told by more then a few folks when she drank that she was "crazy."

So with ten years of hurt and guilt locked up inside, Alex Harvey grabbed a guitar and unlocked the door. "She was 41, and her daddy still calls her baby. All the folks around Brownsville say she's crazy."

Larry Collins, feeling the power of the song being born, grabbed the guitar and said to Alex, "Let me show you how to play that."

Twenty minutes later. "Delta Dawn" was finished.

Alex was the first person to record the song, with Tracy Nelson singing on the record.

Bette Midler was a fan of Tracy Nelson and was present one night when Alex and Tracy performed the song. She expressed interest in the song and would record it in time, but it would be recorded for the second time by Helen Redding and then by a young girl named Tanya Tucker. Both versions would chart, and Alex and Larry would win a Grammy for the song. It has been recorded at least 78 times so far.

Some say that there is salvation and redemption in song-writing. I am sure that is probably true. For Alex Harvey, "Delta Dawn" would be a way of both seeing his mom and knowing that she was in a better place. It was his way of letting the world know that his momma wasn't crazy but just a free spirit that was way ahead of her time in the small town of Brownsville, Texas where she worked.

"Now did I hear you say he was a meeting you here today. To take you to His mansion in the sky."

In the Ghetto

On a cold and gray Chicago mornin'
A poor little baby child is born
in the ghetto.

Chapter 7

Mac Davis

IN THE GHETTO

Mac Davis was born January 21st in Lubbock, Texas. In high school, Mac came to realize that he wasn't big enough to have a future in football or boxing. Mac fought in the Golden Gloves at 5'9" tall. Mac moved to Atlanta, Georgia to live with his mom to find out what life outside of Lubbock looked like. After settling into Atlanta, Mac formed a rock n' roll band called the Zots. The Zots would release two singles on OEK records.

The pop world was in LA, so that is where Mac would need to be. After making the move from Atlanta, he soon found a publishing deal writing for Nancy Sinatra's company.

One of the songs he wrote in 1968, "A Little Less Conversation," went on to be recorded by Elvis Presley, and eventually

"A father to the fatherless, defender of widows, is God in His Holy dwelling."
Psalm 68:5

became a radio hit after Elvis' death in 1977.

The year 1968 in America was a powder keg waiting to be lit with racial unrest and a lingering war in Vietnam. All of this was being played out on pop radio. Protest songs sprang up everywhere. Groups like The Birds, The Mama's and The Papa's, Bob Dylan, and others were establishing themselves as mainstream folk and pop heroes for the modern day cause back then.

The Beatles had taken over the top spot on the pop charts, and Elvis had been making his string of successful movies filled with songs to promote the movies. Those songs filled his pockets with plenty of money but left his heart and soul empty with a lack of meaningful material.

Mac was moved by the plight of the young black man growing up without a dad because the father had either run off, was in jail, or had died from street violence.

A song title came to Mac called, "Vicious Circle." He was trying to come up with a feel for the song idea when one day the "Honky Tonk Angels" would pay him a visit. This time they were cleverly disguised as Freddy Weller, who at the time was playing with the hit group Paul Revere and the Raiders.

While sitting in the publishing office of Nancy Sinatra's at Music 9000 Sunset Boulevard, Freddy showed Mac a new guitar lick he had learned from Tony Joe White, "Polk Salad Annie."

Right about that time, the network news covering the racial riots in Detroit and Chicago had dubbed the inner city areas involved "The Ghetto."

Add one very cool guitar lick compliments of Freddy Weller and Tony Joe White to one new and catchy term from the media press corps along with a little help from God, and there it was... "In the Ghetto."

After Mac Davis had written the tender ode that reflected the sometimes sad life of the African American in 1968, he received a call from Priscilla Presley. Elvis was in need of songs that would be more along the lines of earlier Elvis success. He was ready to record what he wanted, and not what the movie executives felt were needed to go with the movies he had been cranking out like Buick's in Detroit.

Mac's song, "Memories," had been a huge hit for Elvis, so they decided to go back to the well again.

Mac sent eleven songs to the King of Rock and Roll. The first song on the tape was "In The Ghetto," which would go to #2 on the charts, and the second song was another heartfelt ballad that Elvis could not pass up called "Don't Cry Daddy," which would reach the top of the charts and be a big part of the Elvis comeback. Life has often covered many a canvas of the creative person, and sometimes that canvas paints a bleak picture. At least someone had come along and made a voice for those who were suffering and were desperately wanting to be heard....in the ghetto.

Bernie and Mac Davis at Noshville Restaurant in Nashville 2015

A Little Good News

Nobody fired a shot in anger,
nobody had to die in vain.
We sure could use a little
good news today...

Chapter 8

Charlie Black

Rory Bourke

A LITTLE GOOD NEWS

In Mark 16:15, Jesus, after His resurrection, told the apostles to go out into the world and preach "The Good News." If Christ were to tell disciples to do that today, it might be a bit of a project to fulfill.

Tommy Rocco

Good News—who wants to hear that? Gloom and doom, gloom and doom is what sells. Somebody shot somebody else, or someone famous is going to jail, or maybe a big story about war or fear of war. Yeah! That's what everyone wants to hear these days. "Preach the good word?" Good luck getting any

49

"The mouth speaks that which the heart is full of."
Luke 6-45

takers for that newspaper these days.

Well, that was the sentiment in 1983 for three seasoned songwriters, Tommy Rocco, Rory Bourke, and Charlie Black. We'll get back to them in a minute.

Anne Murray would most likely have been very good as a physical education teacher in her hometown of Summerside, Prince Edward Island, Nova Scotia. However, music was deeply rooted in her DNA and wasn't going away anytime too soon. She had tried out for the syndicated Canadian television show *Singalong Jubilee* several times and eventually landed a role in the show after two failed attempts. She was barely into her first year as a teacher when she was approached by the show's producer, Brian Ahern, to move to Toronto and record a solo record on the Arc Record label in 1968. After a year on the Arc label, she switched to Capitol Records to record her sophomore project, "This Way Is My Way."

The record would find a single with a B-side called "Snowbird" that somehow (Hello Honky Tonk Angels) would start getting a lot of radio spins that lead to it becoming a huge record. "Snowbird" would be Anne Murray's first #1 hit in Canada and reach #8 on the US Billboard Top 100 Chart as well.

After several number #1's and a slew of TV appearances on such huge shows as the Glen Campbell Show, Anne did the unthinkable. She stepped away from her career to raise her new family with her husband and record producer, Bill Langstroth, shortly after the birth of their son Will in 1975.

Leave it to those pesky angels to relight the fire that was originally Anne Murray's. It's a good thing for us that she did and an even better thing for the writing team of Tommy Rocco,

Rory Bourke, and Charlie Black.

Tommy Rocco, "Right or Wrong" by George Strait, Charlie Black "Come Next Monday" by KT Oslin, and Rory Bourke, "The Most Beautiful Girl In The World" by Charlie Rich sat down to write one day in 1982.

Like most co-writes, the idea of what to write was discussed. The current news back then much like today was a steady diet of nothing but "bad" news. A Korean jet liner had recently crashed killing all on board and along with the political agendas and price of gas that was a ridiculous $1.25 per gallon, there was no "good" news to be found.

Rory Bourke sounded off, "What this country needs is a little good news." And with that, the three hit songwriters put their #2 pencils to work and set off constructing what would become Anne Murray's 7th #1 country hit.

Rory told me something that I have heard hundreds of times over the years, "The song kind of wrote itself." Wow, how can that be? Songs don't actually write themselves, do they? "It's almost as if the words were already there." I hear that so many times with the great songs.

When God wants something to be said, He finds a way to get His message out.

I think that God was feeling the need to let people know that there is plenty of "good news" out there. It's just that the media doesn't see a profit from spreading it around although God does. The Good News as Christ suggested in Mark 15:16 is still there for those that need to hear it. It feels like you took a long, hot shower after hearing something with an uplifting value to it. Don't be surprised if one day you find yourself writing a song about more positive news or just spreading some around. God likes that.

Love in the First Degree

Lock me away inside of your love
and throw away the key. I'm guilty,
of love in the first degree...

Chapter 9

Jim Hurt

Tim Dubois

LOVE IN THE FIRST DEGREE

It has always amused me the way that God's angels some-times use unfortunate circumstances to achieve their goals. When I heard the story of a struggling songwriter that moved to Nashville posing as an accountant at an established firm, the inspiration behind his first number one hit, and how it involved a convicted murderer, I tracked him down to hear his version of it first hand.

Nobody that is anybody in the music world doesn't know who Tim Dubois is these days.

Tim moved to Nashville in 1977 and soon landed positions in both the songwriting world as a staff writer at House of Gold that was run by hit producer Bob Montgomery, and as

"We love because He
loved us first."
1 John 4-19

a professor in accounting at several universities including Vanderbilt and Tennessee State University.

While Tim was learning his craft at songwriting veteran producer, Harold Shedd, was developing a beach band out of Ft. Payne, Alabama named Wild Country, only a few blocks away from Tim's writing room on Music Row. The band was soon to be signed to RCA after changing their name to Alabama having charted success with their song "Tennessee River."

Tim was in that place where all writers start off - wondering when their first break would come, and was sitting in his car at the corner of 12th Avenue and Edgehill when he heard on the radio that some poor individual had been found guilty of murder in the first degree.

Now, in case you didn't know, songwriters are wired a little different than most people, and words are often what puts a thought into motion for a song. A simple phrase can be twisted around to fit something in their heads. They take words, chew them up in their minds, and flip them around until they find the turn of phrase they are looking for to make a song title a little different from others.

While sitting in his car on the street corner a few blocks from his publisher's office, he came up with the title "Love In The First Degree."

Tim headed straight over to his writing room at House of Gold where he met up with the veteran writer, Jim Hurt. A few hours later, they walked away with the basic outlay of the song. Tim worked on the song until he finally had it hammered out to the finished version.

Of course, it would need a demo, so Jim Hurt recorded it on

the next session he had coming up.

Tim was excited about the freshness of the song and was anxious to see what the boss, Bob Montgomery, was going to think of it in the weekly song review meeting.

To say the least, it was not the exuberant response he was expecting. Bob said that it was different and more or less passed on it. So the song went into the song cassette witness protection plan for a while, sitting on a shelf in a rapidly increasing pile of other songs at House of Gold Publishing.

The engineer on the session that the song was demoed on was a guy by the name of Ben Hall, and Ben was friends with Harold Shedd (stay with me here, Alabama's producer), and Ben really liked the song.

Months would go by since the day they recorded the demo, and it was obvious that Tim's publisher wasn't going to pitch the song.

On a fall day while raking leaves at his house, Tim was informed by his wife that Ben Hall was on the phone. Now, why in the world would Ben Hall be calling Tim Dubois on a Saturday? Tim recalls that in those days most phones still had a long coil cord, and Tim's kids were being kids and were making too much noise for him to be able to hear anything on the phone. Tim stretched the phone cord as far as he could until he was outside on the deck of the house.

Once Tim finally was able to hear Ben, he asked what was up. Ben shouted over the phone, "Listen to this." Tim couldn't make out what it was that he was listening to, so he asked Ben what it was. Ben told him that it was "Love In The First Degree." At first, Tim didn't even remember the song as it had gotten buried in his backlog of songs that were turned in since he first demoed it. Once he recalled the song, he asked Ben who was singing it.

"Alabama," Ben said.

Well, that was nice, but the group was still in its infant stages and were barely a name heard around Nashville. But Tim was thankful for the cut and soon would come to realize that this little cut would become a very big, life-changing thing for both him and his family.

Back then, records usually would have two singles and then move on to the next record and a new single off that new record. However, Alabama was getting pretty busy touring with their new found success, so they hadn't had time to get back into the studio and finish what they were hoping would be a hit on their next record, *Mountain Music*. The record label, RCA, decided to go ahead with an unprecedented third single. "Love In The First Degree" would go on to be Alabama's third #1 and would cross over into the pop music charts establishing them as a real powerhouse in the music world.

It would also give a dreamer a taste of his long sought after dream; a hit song on the country music charts. I'm not sure what became of that poor soul found guilty of a horrible crime, but I do know that Tim Dubois would not only go on to write such great songs as "When I Call Your Name" for Vince Gill and Jerry Reed's "She Got The Gold Mine I Got The Shaft." He would also start one of Nashville's most respected management companies, Fitzgerald /Hartley. He would also be tagged to run Clive Davis' new country version of his pop label, Arista, and would launch the careers of Brooks and Dunn, Pam Tillis, and Alan Jackson just to name a few.

Honky Tonk Angels are very real if you ask me, and they have long-range plans that we can't see right away. They started off small by putting a twist on words into the mind of a songwriter while sitting in his car considering whether he should move his family back to Texas. It also proves to me that God does so love to see our dreams come true, and that He does love us—and that it's a love in the first degree.

I'll Think of Something

I don't know how I'll get her off my mind, but give me time and I'll think of something...

Chapter 10

Bill Rice

Jerry Foster

I'LL THINK OF SOMETHING

Ilove when country songs that I listened to when I was younger find a home with other artists years later.

For that matter, I truly believe that the really great songs
find new homes long after they were hits on someone else.

"I'll Think Of Something" is just such a song. I have no
doubt that it will get recorded again in the future.

Jerry Foster was raised the son of a hard-working Missouri farmer. When he was old enough to enlist, Jerry joined
the Marines. While performing one night at a club off base
in Beauford, South Carolina, he was discovered by a local car
dealership owner and started doing shows with the car dealer's
help. That soon landed him on the then popular Peach State
Jamboree.

Foster got his first record deal with Houston-based Back Beat Records, which was run by Don Robey and later absorbed by ABC Records in 1970.

Wilbur Steven "Bill" Rice was raised in Arkansas and was doing well as an artist himself when he would have a fateful meeting with a young Missouri songwriter/artist named Jerry Foster in 1961. That meeting would change both of their lives for decades to come. Both Rice and Foster were performing and touring as artists when they compared self-penned material.

Jerry Foster tells me that when Rice heard his songs, he mentioned that Jerry's lyrics were great, but that his melodies all sounded somewhat similar. Foster allowed Rice to try his hand at a better melody for one of his songs and soon after, a classic songwriting team was born.

Bill Hall and Cowboy Jack Clements both played a role in Foster and Rice's success before they made their move to Nashville in 1967 and afterward as well. The two at the time had a publishing company based out of Beaumont, Texas. Foster and Rice would see their first cut with legendary artist Charley Pride with the 1968 song, "The Day The World Stood Still." They would continue to get songs recorded by artists such as Jerry Lee Lewis, "Would You Take A Chance On Me," "Thirty-Nine And Holding," and Mickey Gilley's "Here Comes That Hurt Again."

They set up writing sessions every day in an office off 16th Avenue across from the old Mercury Records building.

After writing one day, the two parted ways with Jerry staying in Nashville, and Bill returning to his home 35 miles west of town in Dickson, Tennessee.

Jerry told me that he had been talking to a friend that had made evening plans for a date with three girls on the same night (Honky Tonk Angels no doubt). Jerry asked the guy, "What are you going to do if all three girls show up?"

He said his friend smiled and said, "I don't know, but I'll think of something!"

Knowing a hit idea when he heard one, Jerry got on the phone and called his buddy Bill Rice. He told him that he needed to come back to Nashville and write this idea he had.

"Don't you think it can wait until tomorrow, Jerry?" Rice asked.

"No," replied Jerry.

Well, a short 45-minute drive later the two were knee-deep into this new song that seemed to "write itself."

Jerry told me that the office they were writing in had an overnight janitor that was usually cleaning the place that time of night. As they were making the final tweaks on the song, there was a knock on the door. Assuming it was the night janitor, Jerry told Rice that he would dismiss the guy and get back to finishing the song. When he opened the door, both Rice and Foster were surprised to find Jim Vienneau, who was then the head of MGM Records and producer of Hank Williams, Jr.

Vienneau was quick to the point. He said that while the two veteran writers were working on their new song, he could hear every word since it was channeled through the air conditioning duct right into his office. He was working late because he was frantically trying to find a hit for the Hank, Jr. session the next morning. He told Jerry and Bill to put a simple work tape on his desk when they were done and to slip the lyrics under his door in the morning, and that he would record it the next day on Hank, Jr.

Now, I can tell you that I live in Dickson, Tennessee and as much as I enjoy distancing myself from the craziness of Music Row by 35 miles, I don't like making the drive more than once a day. So I could easily see how Bill Rice could have told Jerry Foster that he didn't want to come back into town to write Jerry's new idea, but something told him to make that drive.

Now, let's pretend that Bill had stayed in Dickson that night and waited until the next day to write the song with Jerry Foster. I'm confident the two would have probably written that same song, but the opportunity that God had prepared would have been missed.

His timing was perfect. He made it possible for Hank Williams' producer to hear the song as it was being written; that same producer who just so happened to be in need of a "miracle" song that night.

Fast forward to 1992. Mark Chesnutt was 11 years old in his hometown of Beaumont, Texas when Hank, Jr. released his version of "I'll Think Of Something," but it must have left a lasting impression. Mark put the song into his live show years later and when discovered by Mark Wright for his first record deal, it was agreed that Chesnutt needed to record a new version of the country classic. It would be a #1 on Chesnutt, and renew young listeners with the powerful melody and haunting lyrics of Jerry Foster and Bill Rice's 18-year-old song all over again. How does a young man of nineteen know much about such things?

Now, to me, that is nothing short of an act of God. He knew that Mark Chesnutt would be heard in a Honky Tonk years later performing, and that he would need to be singing "I'll Think Of Something" to seal the deal.

What we sometimes perceive as acts of coincidence are in fact God's timing at work in our lives.

Now, I don't know how the date with three different girls worked out for Jerry Foster's overzealous friend, but I do know that if God were ever in a bind, He would think of something.

I'll Think Of Something

Goodbye Time

And if its too late for love to change
your mind, then its goodbye time...

Chapter 11

James Dean Hicks

Roger Murrah

GOODBYE TIME

Growing up, I always thought that all couples got divorced. Not because mine did or really any of my friends for that matter, but it was all that was on country radio back then. Cheating songs and songs about break-ups were the norms with artists such as George Jones, Loretta Lynn, Merle Haggard, and Conway Twitty.

Conway was well known for songs about infidelity or heartache. My question is: How does a young man still in his teens know about such things let alone be able to put them into the words of a song?

James Dean Hicks made the trip south from Kentucky in the mid 80's and like so many others before and after him,

"The end of a matter is better than the beginning, and patience is better than pride."
Ecclesiastes 7-8

didn't know a soul.

He got a small efficiency apartment just off Music Row and started going through the phone book calling publishers. He saw the name Tom Collins Music and thought, "Hey I know who he is!" and proceeded to find his way to the Tom Collins office on the Row. He met song plugger Rich Alves and played him a few songs, which then led to James Dean being put in front of Tom Collins to play songs for him. Collins was impressed enough to offer the young Mr. Hicks a place to write and the prospect of a possible publishing deal in the future. Not being a staff writer, James would have to write anywhere he could, bathrooms, vocal booths, and wherever he could find an empty room. He also spent many nights asking Mr. Collins about songwriting, hoping to hone his yet undeveloped skills.

Now being naive has never been fortuitous that I'm aware of but in the case of James Dean Hicks, it would soon pay off.

One night while picking the noodle of the already legendary Tom Collins, James asked him if he still wrote songs. Tom said he did but not really all that much. That would prove to be the appropriate moment for James to put his size 8 foot in his mouth. He told Tom Collins that he was a big fan of all the songs he had written for Merle Haggard. Collins looked at the youngster from Kentucky and said,

"You idiot, that's Tommy Collins."

Feeling about as useless as a beer opener at a convent, James figured that his lack of knowledge would surely get him put back on the streets looking for another writing house where he could hang out. Instead, the next day Tom Collins offered

James a publishing deal. James says he thinks it's because he felt sorry for him. Whatever the reason, that new publishing deal would bring James Dean Hicks into the writing circle with Roger Murrah, "It Takes A Little Rain" for The Oak Ridge Boys, and "High Cotton" for Alabama.

How in the heck did I get so far off track from my original thought? Country songs have had their fair share of heartbreak history. Now, as I have said repeatedly, God makes huge use of what we call setbacks or life tragedies. Divorce is a painful life and faith changing ordeal. It will either drive you away from God with bitter thinking that He has abandoned you or increase your faith in Him knowing He is moving heaven and earth on your behalf.

James Dean Hick's brother was going through a divorce and was at the time unable to let go and move on. James was deeply moved by the hurt he saw in his brother. He mentioned it to Roger Murrah during one of their writing sessions, and the idea for "Goodbye Time" was born.

Throughout so many of my interviews for this book, I have heard the same theme, "It's like it wrote itself." My thoughts on that are fairly concrete. The song like all of God's works was predestined. That being said, the songs were already written, and God just showed us the words.

"Goodbye Time" was first pitched to Reba McEntire, but she was in the middle of her own divorce and felt the words to the song were too close to home and passed on recording it.

It didn't take long to find a new home. It was pitched to Conway Twitty and would become a very big hit for him in 1988.

Fast forward sixteen years to 2004. Blake Shelton was raised with Conway Twitty music and if that weren't enough, he and James Dean Hicks had worked together before Blake got his big break. He was always a fan of the song and when the window was there, he recorded it.

The Blake Shelton album *Barn and Grill* would produce other hits as well, like "Some Beach" and "Nobody But Me." The uncanny closeness to the Conway version on Blake's record was amazing and a real tribute to the legendary Mr. Twitty and the writers of the song as well.

God, if nothing else, is patient. His timing is perfect, and even though we don't see Him at work on our behalf, He is always lining things up for us way in advance. Great songs do have a life of their own, and I am sure that "Goodbye Time" will continue to be recorded for generations to come.

GOODBYE TIME

Jose Cuervo

Jose Cuervo, you are a friend of
mine. I like to drink you with a little
salt and lime...

Chapter 12

CINDY JORDAN

Cindy Jordan

JOSE CUERVO

Cynthia Jordan, the author of the hit song "Jose Cuervo," wrote the song for Shelly West. When asked if she really did all the things that she talks about in her song, she always replies, "Of course not, at least not all in one night!"

As a twenty-one-year-old divorced, single mom waiting tables for a living, Cynthia (Cindy) was wondering if this was all that life held in store for her. Not one to have really written a lot of songs, Cindy was not totally aware that a lot of hit writers find that magic sometimes happens in the early hours of the day or as we like to call it, that "Magic Window." There is no justifiable proof that that is when Honky Tonk Angels are at their best, but it has been a pretty good time slot for a lot of

"I called out to the Lord in distress, and He answered me.."

Jonah 2-1-2

great song concepts.

Cindy had finished a shift at Ichabod Crane's in Torrance, California and was waiting for her boyfriend to get home. She poured herself a small glass of Tequila and was listening to her favorite singer-songwriter (heck everyone's favorite singer-songwriter), Kris Kristofferson sing, "On a Sunday morning sidewalk, wishing Lord that I was stoned. For there's something bout a Sunday makes a body feel alone."

Then like Excalibur, her guitar was crying out to her as it leaned against the sofa. Curious to see what her old friend had hidden away, she picked it up and found words that she had no idea were even inside her. "Sunday morning and the sun is shining in my eye that is open and my head is spinning. I look at my feet, and I've still got my boots on. I had too much Tequila last night.

"What the heck is that, and where did it come from?" She wondered.

On the coffee table sat her little glass of Tequila and after taking a sip, she sang, "Jose Cuervo, you are a friend of mine!" and a classic country song was born.

So the next step of getting a rowdy, chick friendly drinking song on the radio shouldn't take any time at all, right?

Besides waiting tables, Chythia was earning fifty dollars a day to wear a bikini and walk the local beach pouring Tequila for customers while wearing a sash for Jose Cuervo. She was hired by Hueblein the parent company of Jose Cuervo. Cindy decided to make a demo of her new song. She found a way to play the song for the Heublein powers that be, but they found no interest in the song. Strike One. Then she heard about a talent contest put on by the local radio station, KLAC. The panel of judges were fairly impressive and included Al Gallico, a big publisher from Nashville. Cindy and her new song made it to the finals but lost the overall contest. Strike Two.

Al Gallico called her the day after the contest to tell her he wanted to sign the song to his company, and that he was sure it was a hit. This was definitely the big break she was looking for. However, Al Gallico played the song for everyone he could think of and was turned down by all of them. As a matter of a fact, most of the people that Al played the song for told him that they thought it was a huge piece of crap. Strike three, game over, adios, close the door on your way out, do not pass go, do not collect two hundred dollars.

You know, I think that Honky Tonk Angels love rejections. I think they love Strike Three. It's like they love pulling for the underdog. Time and time again, they show up when all hope seems gone.

Not really knowing when to give up, Cindy decided to record "Jose Cuervo" herself. Her friend George Anderson at KMPC radio offered to pay for the demo at Quantos Studios. She was introduced to Denny Belfield, who produced the session. Denny brought the original speed of the song up a bit and added what would become a signature lick on the guitar. One of the musicians that day was John Hobbs on piano. Hobbs would go on to play on several big hits like "Does Ft. Worth Ever Cross Your Mind" for George Strait, and "Strawberry Wine" for Deanna Carter. He won a Grammy for producing Vince Gill's "These Days."

After mixing the song and pressing onto a 45, which was a small record back then that spun 45 revolutions per minute, she took the record to a friend of a friend at KLAC radio, Larry Scott, who had a late night radio show. That night after leaving the radio station, Cindy got to experience what every singer dreams of, and that is to hear themselves on the radio for the first time. Cindy wasn't the only person that would hear her on the radio. Andy Wickham from Warner Bros Records had heard the performance one night while riding around after a party he had been to. Al Gallico called her to let her know that Warner Bros. wanted to sign her to a record deal and was flying her to Dallas to meet Stan Byrd, who was the head of promotions for the label.

A first class plane ticket and the red carpet treatment was what Cindy was handed, and she was hoping to be the next big thing. For whatever reason, the song didn't click with Mr. Byrd, and he would not put any promotion behind the record. So just like that, the clock again struck twelve, and Cinderella had no coach, no gown, and her glass slipper was just an old pair of cowboy boots that had beat the pavement everywhere they could to try to keep the song going, but it was over.

Cindy had ridden that roller coaster for so long up and down, up and down that she was emotionally spent. She was broke, her personal life was a mess, and she had lost all hope of success in the music world. One day in her living room back in Torrence, she just let it all go, and God was on the receiving end of her frustration.

"Come on God, really? The heck with you, I pray, I knocked on the door like you said, and this is all I get? You can move mountains, and make the solar system, and you can't even get my record up the charts?"

So Cynthia Jordan gave up and went back to waiting tables, but she did decide to let God have it His way.

Enter guess who? That's right. Now came God time.

John Hobbs, the piano player on Cindy's record, was also playing on a master session for Shelly West, who was coming off a hit duet record with David Frizzell, "You're The Reason

God Made Oklahoma." He had a copy of the song on a cassette. Steve Dorff, songwriter-producer that would write nine #1 movie songs and fifteen top ten country songs, including hits on the George Strait movie Pure Country, was producing the session but didn't feel it was anything more than a novelty song. Hobbs told Dorff that he could get a chart written in a few minutes and suggested they at least try it.

The next week, Al Gallico called Cindy to let her know that Shelly West had cut her song, but Cindy was through getting all excited anymore. The fire was gone, and she wasn't up for another heartbreak.

When you first get a single on the radio, you tend to follow the Billboard charts to see what your song is doing. Expecting yet one more slammed door, she wasn't very impressed when it entered the charts at #73. The next week, though, it started to get interesting. "Jose Cuervo" came in at #53 its second week, a twenty point jump in the charts. It was #43 the third week.

"Come on God don't play with me," she thought. But as we know now, this time the song was rocking on Honky Tonk Angel time and wouldn't stop until it hit the top of the charts.

You know frustration is a part of every songwriter's life in the early days and even later on after much success, we all tend to hit walls that seem unfair and too tall to climb over. When we just finally let go and get out of God's way, that is when the good stuff starts to happen. "Jose Cuervo, you are a friend of mine," and so are those little Tequila-loving angels sometimes.

House At Pooh Corner

Christopher Robin and I walked
along under branches lit up by the
moon...

Chapter 13

Kenny Loggins

HOUSE AT POOH CORNER

Everett, Washington is the birthplace of hit-maker Kenny Loggins. His father would move his family several times across the country before settling in Alhambra, California where he would attend high school at San Gabriel Mission High School, where he graduated in 1966. But let's just leave Kenny in high school for a little bit. Unlike most hit songwriters that would not find their songwriting skills until long after high school, Kenny Loggins would write two of his biggest songs while still a senior at San Gabriel Mission High.

Songwriters in the round at the Bluebird Cafe would not come to be for another twenty-two years, so finding an outlet for playing new songs was a unique problem for a songwriting newbie in 1970. That problem would get solved in the way

"See that you do not despise one of these little ones. For I tell you angels in heaven always see the face of my Father in heaven." Matthew 18-10

of house parties in the surrounding Los Angeles area. At some of those parties, Loggins would make friends with a couple of members of a new group that was about to record their first record. John McEuen and Jeff Hanna were founding members of future Hall Of Fame pop/country group, The Nitty Gritty Dirt Band. Kenny Loggins, at the unbelievably young age of 17, had already written "Danny's Song," Ann Murray Grammy Award winning song and "House At Pooh Corner." The latter was inspired by the 1928 book with the same name written by A.A. Milne.

Loggins claims that he was moved by the thought of the fictional character in the book, Christopher Robin, saying goodbye to his friends at the Hundred Acre Wood.

After playing "House At Pooh Corner" at one of those house parties, John McEuen told Loggins that they really wanted to record the song on their upcoming record-—*Uncle Charlie and His Dog Teddy*, Capitol Records 1970.

Being just a kid fresh out of high school, this was amazing, life changing, and downright pretty groovy as they said back then.

But it would not take long before those illusions of greatness would be crushed with just one phone call.

John McEuen would be the bearer of bad news. The record label that the Nitty Gritty Dirt Band was signed to had been bombarded with threats from the attorneys representing the book *House At Pooh Corner*, which was owned by the Disney Company. End of game.

Enter Honky Tonk Angels 1960's style. That night, Kenny

had a Friday night date, but he informed his girlfriend that he probably wouldn't be much fun. He explained to his young date that he thought he was getting his first ever cut, but it looked like it wasn't going to happen now. While on this fateful date, Loggins was asked by his girlfriend why the cut wasn't going to happen. He explained to her that it was all big business and that corporate Disney had nixed the recording. This is where those hippy, chicky, little Honky Tonk Angels are really at their best.

Unbeknownst to Kenny, his girlfriend's dad was the CEO of Disney. She simply explained to Loggins that she would have a talk with daddy. Are you kidding me?

A few days later Kenny Loggins would get a different kind of phone call from his pal, John McEuen.

The recording was back on thanks to Kenny's girlfriend's convenient closeness to the big dog at Disney.

Not only would Loggins get "House At Pooh Corner" recorded by The Nitty Gritty Dirt Band, but he would get an additional three songs on that Watermark recording. The song would reach #53 on the Billboard charts in June of 1971 and launch the careers of both The Nitty Gritty Dirt Band and Kenny Loggins, who would soon team up with a fellow by the name of Jim Messina. Together they would tear up the music charts in the 70's and 80's as Loggins and Messina.

Now you can call it coincidence that Kenny Loggins just happened to be dating the daughter of a big shot at Disney, and that Loggins would write a song that The Nitty Gritty Dirt Band would want very much to record but couldn't because of legal issues with Disney, but I choose to see it as God just having fun and showing off.

I think God loves children's stories and was particularly fond of this one. So as the saying goes, where there's a will or angels—there's a way.

Lucille

In a bar in Toledo across from the depot, on a bar stool she took off her ring...

Chapter 14

Hal Byrum

Roger Bowling

LUCILLE

Born in Pensacola, Florida, Larry Butler was destined at an early age to be in the music business. Before he was old enough to drive, he performed on *The Red Foley Show*. Later after joining a Florida-based band Jerry Woodward and the Esquires, he would cross paths with publisher Buddy Killen. Killen would encourage Larry to move to Nashville and find his place there. After moving to Twangtown in 1963, he rapidly started lending his fresh piano style to such great hits as Conway Twitty's "Hello Darlin" and Bobby Goldsboro's "Honey." Despite his high demand on multiple star's recordings like John-

"You shall not covet your neighbors house, you shall not covet your neighbors wife..."
Exodus 20-17

ny Cash, George Jones, and Tammy Wynette, he decided that the new Memphis sound was where he needed to be. So in the late 60's, he made the timely move that would team him up with Memphis songster Chips Moman. Larry would soon join the group the Gentry's and have huge success with songs like "Keep On Dancing" and "Every Day I Have To Cry Some."

Larry Butler was touring and recording with a big pop act and enjoying success in the middle of the 60's music explosion. But God had only begun to use Larry's talents, and He had much bigger plans for him a lot further down the road about 200 miles east of Memphis, Tennessee.

When in Nashville In the early 70's, anybody who was anybody from Elvis to the Beatles stayed at the world famous Spence Manor. Webb Pierce would forever make it one of Nashville's most unique hotels by having a guitar-shaped swimming pool built next to it.

Shortly after their paths would cross, Spence Manor would play a very large role in the success of Larry Butler and up-and-coming songwriter, Roger Bowling.

Roger Bowling had tried his hand on Music Row in 1970 but found all the doors in "Hitsville" closed to him. He knew that he didn't have the right songs to get anyone's attention, so he packed up his things and returned to his stomping grounds in Harlan, Kentucky.

Four years later would find Roger back making the rounds on those two famous one-way streets that make up Music Row. This time with a fresh bag of songs, he would start to see success after meeting Larry Butler, who had moved back to Nashville to head up United Artists records. Butler liked a few of Roger's songs and soon recorded "Pour It All On Me" on veteran artist Del Reeves.

Roger Bowling was a likable guy. He and Butler would spend time together outside of the UA record office.

If you wanted a poker game in Nashville, it wasn't hard to find one back then. Long before Facebook and multi-channel television, poker games were the precursor to the "Man Cave."

The best place to find a poker game and hang out was Spence Manor.

A few years down the road, Larry Butler and Kenny Rogers would share the prized CMA Awards stage for Song Of The Year with "The Gambler," but maybe he could have used some of the lyrics from that song the night that his new writer from Kentucky and a few of his other Nashville cronies were playing poker at Spence Manor.

Larry had recently married and was pretty sure that his new bride would not understand that he needed to pay his new songwriter, Roger Bowling, four thousand dollars after losing a big hand to him.

You remember those lyrics, "You've got to know when to hold 'em, know when to fold 'em."

Surely there was something that they could work out. After all, Larry was a hit producer, and Roger was a struggling songwriter looking for big cuts. Roger suggested that Butler record a handful of his songs on a few of his UA artists.

Well, that all sounded like a win-win for both of them, but there was just one snag. The one song that Roger Bowling really wanted to have Larry record broke all the rules of record label head, Billy Sherrill. It was a waltz for one, a huge taboo back then, and pretty much true today. It was also over four minutes long. If that wasn't enough to sink the deal, it was a song that painted a woman in a not too favorable light; a song about a woman that was trying to pick up a total stranger in a bar.

This was not just any bar, but "a bar in Toledo, across from the depot." That's right, Roger Dale Bowling and fellow co-writer, Hal Byrum, had written a true classic country song, "Lucille."

Larry Butler felt that it was a pretty good song with a catchy hook, but there was no way to get it past the parameters of seasoned veteran record head, Billy Sherrill.

Facing the uncomfortable alternative of explaining to his new, but not too understanding, bride that he had dropped four thousand dollars in a poker game, Larry did the unthinkable; he cut "Lucille" hoping that his instincts were right about the song. He decided to track it on a pop artist that was pretty much on his last leg with the record label. Kenny Rogers and the First Edition had seen notable success with pop hits like "Ruben James" and "Just Dropped In To See What Condition My Condition Was In," but the times they were a-changing. The acid and pot-laced song days were just about gone, and Kenny Rogers would either make it as a country artist or go the way of the Schwinn banana seat bike with a sissy bar.

Wow, you talk about a lot of major pieces that had to fall into place to make a song that the label didn't want. It was written by a fairly untested songwriter and recorded on a down and out pop icon, but for Honky Tonk Angels it was a pretty simple task. "Lucille" would go on to be the CMA Song of the Year for 1977. It would also open the door for Kenny Rogers, who would become one of the biggest country stars of all time.

Songwriting is always a gamble. The chances of holding a winning hand are always slim at best. But when Honky Tonk Angels are dealing the cards, the deck will always be stacked in your favor.

LUCILLE

The Gambler

On a warm summer's eve on a train bound for nowhere, I met up with a gambler we were both too tired to sleep....

Chapter 15

DON SCHLITZ

Don Schlitz

THE GAMBLER

You couldn't put three more different people together to make one country classic than the song "The Gambler," not to mention the unexpected appeal to millions of people loving a drunk, washed-up gambler on a train.

Honky Tonk Angels went way overboard on this one. The idea of a former Memphis pop artist producing a former jazz singer from Houston on a song written by a third shift computer tech from Durham, North Carolina... Go Duke!

Their paths would collide in 1978 but would start long before that in Houston, Texas on August 21, 1938 when Mr. Kenny Rogers was born. He would launch into the music world

"For what will it profit a man if he gains the whole world and loses his own soul?"

Mark 8-36

playing a variety of bands throughout the 50's and 60's, including a jazz group before landing a backup singer/ bass player gig with the New Christie Minstrels in 1963. Wanting to be more in line with the modern acid rock scene of the late 60's, he and other band members, Mike Settle, Terry Williams, and Thelma Camacho left the Minstrels and formed the First Edition. They were later joined by Kin Vassey and renamed Kenny Rogers and the First Edition. They would splatter the charts with hits like, "Ruben James," "But You Know I Love You," and "Ruby Don't Take Your Love To Town."

Despite their success, the group broke up in 1976 with Rogers pursuing a solo career. Hold that thought for a minute.

While Kenny Rogers was going through bands like Sheridan through Richmond, Larry Butler was pretty much doing the same thing. After leaving his hometown of Pensacola, Florida in the 50's, he would go in and out of several bands before meeting legendary publisher Buddy Killen in Nashville in 1963. He would leave a few years later; even though, he was in high demand as a session player on records for Conway Twitty and other artists like Loretta Lynn. Moving to Memphis, he joined the group, The Gentry's, and had big pop hits like "Keep On Dancing," and "Every Day I Have To Cry Some."

While those two were sowing their musical roots all over the country, Don Schlitz was being born in Durham, North Carolina in 1952. It would be twenty-six years before the three of them would create country music history, but I have no doubt that God had that all figured out way back then.

Don Schlitz had made the trek to Nashville in the early 70's and found refuge under the wing of veteran hit song maker Bob McDill, "Amanda," "Good Old Boys Like Me," and "He's Gone Country." McDill found some magic hidden in Schlitz's early attempts at songwriting and would write with the new kid on the block allowing some of the good stuff to rub off.

One afternoon after leaving McDill's office and walking back to his apartment not far from Music Row, Don wrote what would be the bulk of "The Gambler." It took him another six weeks of kicking around options of how to end the song that he came up with the verse about the wise, advice-giving gambler to "break even and die in his sleep."

After hearing it on the radio after all these now 40 years, you would have thought that it would have been cut by someone and made a hit the very next day after Don wrote it.

That's what I love about Honky Tonk Angels. They have an agenda, and they never waiver from it despite our agony at the time. Despite our empty bank accounts, bald tires, and distaste for crazy late shift jobs to pay for those bald tires, God attempts to teach us patience and His timing. If it weren't for the sheer love of writing songs, all the great writers would have pawned their two hundred dollar guitars for half a tank of gas to get them back to whatever little town they came from.

"The Gambler" would manage what should have been big cuts from both Bobby Bare and Johnny Cash. Success on either one of those great country crooners was not meant to be.

It would be two years after Don wrote the song, twenty-six years after Larry Butler had lit out of Pensacola, and twenty years after Kenny Rogers would leave a jazz band called the Bobby Doyle Three that the song would end up on the top of the country charts.

My old friend since gone, Merlin Littlefield, was one of the best friends a song could have. Without any concern for compensation, Merlin was always out there running songs around trying to find them a home, not as a publisher or song plugger for a publishing company, but as a rep for the Performing Rights Organization, ASCAP. He was aware of the song by way of Don Schlitz's version on his record. He was also aware of the other versions that were out there by Bobby Bare and Johnny Cash. So with a cassette in hand, Littlefield went to Larry Butler's office on 17th Avenue, a short walk down the street from the old ASCAP building at the top of Music Row. He gave the song to Larry and expressed his thoughts that if Kenny Rogers were to record it and release it as a single, Kenny Rogers would forever be known as "The Gambler."

Again, I feel so strongly that the timing was in perfect alignment. Had Kenny not had a hit with "Lucille," which by the way was Kenny Rogers' mother's name, had Johnny Cash singled the song, or Bobby Bare for that matter, the song would not have been perfect for Kenny Rogers.

Perfect song with the perfect voice at the perfect time. Perfectly orchestrated by God.

"And somewhere in the darkness the gambler he broke even. And in his final words, I found an ace that I could keep."

The Gambler

Fishing in the Dark

You and me going fishing in the dark, lying on our backs and counting the stars just moving slow...

Chapter 16

Jim Photoglo

Wendy Waldman

FISHING IN THE DARK

*B*oy's Life magazine suggests in an article about fishing in the dark that fish react differently at night to bait than in the daytime. It explains that fish have tiny nerve endings in their face that work like sonar and pick up movement. So the best chance to catch more fish at night is to keep your bait moving to attract the fish. Good to know.

I have always believed that some musical groups have no real boundaries to their music despite their original roots. The Nitty Gritty Dirt Band has lead the way from its early beginnings in 1966 as a bridge between contemporary rock and traditional country music. When they reached across the aisle, so to speak, to make the landmark record, *Will The Circle Be*

"Immediately they left their nets and followed Him."

Matthew 4:20

Unbroken in 1972, they established themselves as true pioneers in country rock music. With songs on the record with such country legends as Mother Maybelle Carter, Doc Watson, Merle Travis, and Roy Acuff, to name a few, the band was destined to be a game changer in both the rock and country worlds.

Although the band has gone through dozens of band member changes since its early days and shifted away from its acoustic jug band sound to a more electric rock sound, it always remained true to its country flavored music.

In 1987, the band consisted of original founding members Jeff Hanna and Jimmie Fadden with Bob Carpenter on piano and Jimmy Ibbotson on guitars and additional lead vocals.

Jim Photoglo spent the early part of the 1980's living and performing as a solo pop artist in California. With two charted singles of his own, "We Were Meant To Be Lovers" in 1980 and "The Fool In Love With You" in 1981, he had already established himself as a talented writer.

Wendy Waldman grew up in a very musical family. Her father, Fred Steiner, was a composer for such TV shows as *Gunsmoke, Rocky, Bullwinkle*, and *Star Trek*, while her grandfather, George Steiner, wrote music for Laurel and Hardy and the comic strip character Betty Boop. So the idea of sitting around writing music came to Wendy at an early age.

She would write songs for both her own project, "Love Has Got Me" 1973 as well as other artists like Linda Ronstadt, Melissa Manchester, Rita Coolidge, and Bette Midler. By the mid 80's, Wendy was well entrenched in the LA pop scene as a writer, artist, and an emerging producer as well.

Fast forward a few years, and Wendy has been getting songs recorded in Nashville where the twang was starting to come off of some of the records coming out of Nashville. Her hit, "Baby What About You," 1982, opened the door for future cuts there. Jim Photoglo recalled a wedding in LA where he spotted a woman he thought he knew, Wendy Waldman. They struck up a conversation and discovered that they were not only both LA songwriter/artists, but both had had cuts in Nashville. Photoglo just had a title cut on CMA Artist of the Year Gary Morris with "Faded Blue." Wendy mentioned to Jim that she had been going back and forth to Nashville and had a place there. She encouraged him to do the same and offered a sofa to crash on. Photoglo would take her up on the offer and make several three week long visits to Nashville, where he soon found a demand for his songs with several top ten cuts by 1984.

On one of Jim's visits, he got a room at the old Shoney's Inn off Demonbreun Street. He told me that he had been experimenting with melodies that only use the root chord, and what would normally be the third chord or per the Nashville Charts Number System, the 1 and the 5 chords. One morning Jim woke up in the Shoney's Inn room he was at and started playing with the new melody. He recorded two versions of the chord progression using two different melodies over them. He played both versions of the recording for Wendy Waldman. The first version was written by the two of them and recorded by Terri Gibbs, "You Can't Run Away From Your Heart," and later by Kathy Mattea and Patty Loveless as well.

The next time the two of them got together, they had already agreed to write a song using the other melody that Photoglo had come up with that was waiting to be written. When Jim got there, he found out that Wendy had been listening to the radio show Prairie Home Companion. She said to Jim,

"We should write a song about fishing."

Jim told me that his first thought was to run away quickly. Then, she suggested that the song be about fishing in the dark. The song was written fairly quickly and was demoed at Wendy's little eight-track studio. The demo was then played for Wendy's good friend, Josh Leo, who had just been given the project to record the Nitty Gritty Dirt Band's new record on Warner Brothers.

It was never meant to be a big song. It was just two LA writers having fun with a fresh new melody. It was recorded by the Nitty Gritty Dirt Band and would reach the number one spot on country radio. To date, it has reached the five million airplay status and remains one of the most played songs in the history of country music.

Now you can say that it was just good timing that two non-country writers would move to Nashville and write a song about fishing, which, by the way, is not a very common thing out in Los Angeles. I believe that Honky Tonk Angels were definitely using the right bait when they lured the two of them away from the comforts of Los Angeles and onto those two one way streets in Nashville, Tennessee. Or could it be that the fisher of men likes a good song about fishing and was more than happy to make it all happen? "Stayin' the whole night thru, feels so good to be with you."

Brotherly Love

We shared the same last name and the same color eyes. But we fought like tigers over that ol' red bike....

Chapter 17

Jimmy Stewart

Tim Nichols

BROTHERLY LOVE

Many times, songwriters have felt like they had hit the bottom of the bucket.

Well for one future Hall Of Fame songwriter, literally hitting the bottom of the bucket was a Godsend.

Tim Nichols was born in Portsmouth, Virginia, but his family moved between there and Springfield, Missouri. After high school, he took a broadcasting class in college that might have spun him into a totally different field had the school not dropped the program. From there, he found himself "at the bottom of the bucket." Working at a manufacturing plant making

"and in your godliness,
brotherly kindness,
and in your brotherly
kindness, love."
Peter 1:7

buckets for KFC is a pretty good place to take a hard look at your life and find a better path for your future.

Tim took guitar lessons and soon formed a band. A man approached his band, who as it turned out ended up being a scam artist who took their money. Nichols took the case to the Attorney General's office, and he and his band were soon featured on *60 Minutes*. That exposure would get him interest from Nashville, and he and the boys soon packed up and crossed the Mason-Dixon line into Tennessee. By 1984, Tim had landed a publishing deal with Ronnie Milsap's company. Okay, so far Honky Tonk Angels had moved Tim and his family clear across the country, had his broadcasting class canceled, and then put him in a dead end job making those buckets for KFC that would hold Extra Crispy and Original Colonel Sanders chicken. If that wasn't enough of a push in the right direction, they sent a scam artist to con him and his band out of their dream money, only to end up on 60 Minutes being watched by seventy million people. So that's Tim side of the story. We'll get back to him in a minute.

I met Jimmy Stewart somewhere around 1987. He, Tony Arata, "The Dance," Garth Brooks, D. Scott Miller, "To Think I Used To Worry," Delbert McClinton, and I started playing Douglas Corner Cafe on a regular basis every week and became known as The Songwriter Fiasco.

We considered ourselves as the B Team to the big boys playing The Bluebird Cafe back then.

Jimmy is from a dot-in-the-road town about seventy miles west of Nashville called Camden. It is really close to the Tennessee River, and that makes it accessible to a cool place called

Paris, Tennessee.

Jimmy eventually started playing gigs there with his band "The Tennessee River Crooks Band."

However, unless you lived with your mom and dad and never ate, there would not be enough money playing local gigs to pay for much. So Stewart got a job at the Holley carburetor plant.

After recording at a local studio, the band's record fared well selling over a thousand records and getting fair airplay on the area radio stations.

As I have mentioned before, tragedy all too often is brought into our lives to direct us to where God needs us to be. The band's lead guitarist, Ronnie Waters, was suddenly killed which left the band devastated.

The Tennessee River Crooks would go through a series of guitar players after his death, and even gain interest from the legendary band Lynard Skynard. However, the clock was ticking and in 1984, Jimmy Stewart eventually decided to roll east to Music Row.

Jimmy Stewart and Tim Nichols would get together to write not long after they first met. They had written a few times together but hadn't hit the big one yet. Jimmy's brother, Ricky, was the drummer in the Tennessee River Crooks but had some back issues and back then, the doctors didn't regulate how many prescriptions they gave their patients for pain and such. Jimmy's brother had been on a downward spiral abusing the pain pills, and Stewart was pretty worried about him.

The two writers met to see what would fall out, and Jimmy was telling Tim about his concerns for his brother Ricky. Nichols told Stewart that he had an idea he had wanted to write, but he couldn't find anyone that wanted to write it with him. Tim sang the opening line to a song he had in his head, "They share the same last name and the same color eyes."

Stewart, like so many other great writers, was ready to jump in and immediately spouted out, "But they fought like tigers over that old red bike."

Jimmy told me that he really believed the song was written in less than thirty minutes.

It was originally pitched to Ronnie Milsap but having been an orphan, he didn't have any siblings, so the song was not appealing to him. Eventually, Stewart's song pluggers got the song to Jerry Kennedy, who produced Moe Bandy. Bandy recorded the song, but his version of it only reached #53 on the Country Billboard charts. The song had also been recorded by Keith Whitley, while Blake Mevis was recording a possible duet record on him. Mevis was replaced by Garth Fundis, who went on to record the classic "Don't Close Your Eyes" on Whitley. After the tragic death of Keith, Fundis took the track and recorded a duet version with Earl Thomas Conley. The single went all the way to #2 and would forever be a piece of Keith Whitley music history.

It is truly sad to wonder what would have become of Keith had he not died so young in his career and life, but the Honky Tonk Angels were always close to him. The same goes for these two amazing writers who through adversities and struggles, found themselves in a writing room one day to discuss and write their mutual feelings for their brothers.

Don't Close Your Eyes

I know you loved him, a long time ago, but even now in my arms, you still want him I know.....

Chapter 18

BOB McDILL

Bob McDill

DON'T CLOSE YOUR EYES

I have always believed that the difference between a singer and an artist is that a singer sings the song, while an artist interprets it. There have been a number of legendary artists over the years. Hank Williams, George Jones, Tammy Wynette, and Johnny Cash to name but a few. During the 80's and 90's, few country artists would impact the lives of the next generation of singers the way that Keith Whitley would.

Born Jackie Keith Whitley July 1, 1955, in Ashland, Kentucky, Keith would find his way in and out of several bands in the Kentucky area. In 1969, with his brother Dwight on the

"Let the word of Christ
dwell in you richly, singing
psalms, and hymns, and
spiritual songs."
Colossians 3:16

banjo, he entered a contest in Ezel, Kentucky. Also competing in the contest was a Mandolin whiz kid named Ricky Skaggs. The two young men would strike up a lifelong friendship.

Enter Honky Tonk Angels in the way of car troubles. Ralph Stanley would arrive late for a show in Ft. Gay, West Virginia due to a flat tire. When he arrived, he heard what he thought were the Stanley Brothers singing on the jukebox. Much to his surprise, he found a fifteen-year-old Keith Whitley and a sixteen-year-old Ricky Skaggs playing live. Both boys were brought on board to play in Mr. Stanley's band.

After a stint with J.D. Crow and the New South, Whitley found his way to Nashville in 1983 with the hopes of becoming a new voice there.

The origin of the term Honky Tonk is disputed. It is thought to have come from a group of cowboys on their way to a variety show and happened to see a flock of geese on the way. It goes back as far as the late 1890's. A brand of piano bearing a similar name that was played in dance halls in Texas may also be the culprit for this colorful name. Whatever its origin, it was best exemplified in country music in the 1980's. No one came close to being the King of Honky Tonk the way that Keith Whitley did.

Keith signed a record deal with RCA and was originally produced by Norro Wilson and Tony Brown. Blake Chancy would bring Keith onto the country scene with the LA to Miami record, which would garner him respectable charted tracks such as "Miami My Amy" and "Homecoming 63." Keith was touring and finding his sound but hadn't made the record that he felt best defined him as a country artist.

Even back then, the cost of making a 12-track record was expensive and without having been a multi-platinum selling artist, it was hard to recoup the cost for the label. With that said, RCA head honcho and passionate lover of great country music, Joe Galante, The Judds, Martina McBride, Brad Paisley, Vince Gill, and Kenny Chesney asked the young Mr. Whitley to his office on Music Row to discuss the new tracks that were recently recorded. In his mind, Joe was already feeling that the tracks were not going to break any new ground or establish Keith as the superstar that Galante knew he could be. When asked what Whitley thought of the very expensive recordings, Keith told Galante that he wished he could cut new tracks. His thoughts were that the magic songs just weren't there yet.

Joe was glad to see the wisdom from such a new artist and agreed to a new session of songs but wanted to put Whitley with his trusted friend, Garth Fundis, to produce them.

Garth was from Lawrence, Kansas and had a more "rootsier" approach to recording due to his Bluegrass background, and Galante felt they would be a good fit together.

Famous for his recordings with Hall of Fame legend, Don Williams and New Grass Revival, as well as the high, high background vocals on both Don Williams' and Waylon Jennings' versions of the classic, "Amanda," Fundis was twang to the tenth degree. A curious note for me is that "Amanda" was written by one of the greatest country songwriters, Bob McDill. Garth Fundis would go to that deep, deep well one more time for Keith and draw out of it "Don't Close Your Eyes."

I don't know what makes a singer an artist. I think maybe it comes from years of living a life absorbing other people's lives—their highs and lows. I also think that being too good of an observer can put you dangerously close to the fire. Like the Greek legend Icarus that ignored his father's warnings and flew too close to the sun that melted the wax his wings were made of. Keith Whitley definitely flew too high. He lived a life of a country singer and made us all drunk with his intoxicating vocals, but also left himself far too vulnerable to fate.

"Don't Close Your Eyes" would become one of the greatest country records ever made with number one hits off the record, including the title track, "When You Say Nothing At All" and "I'm No Stranger To The Rain." Besides being "No Stranger To The Rain," Keith was no stranger to great country songs. Enter Honky Tonk Angels again. Whitley had recorded several classic country songs before they were made famous by other country greats. He sang "Brother Jukebox," Mark Chesnutt, and "On The Other Hand," Randy Travis, but the angels apparently had different plans for those songs.

Ironically, the man that would allow the budget for those new songs, Joe Galante, would get a copy of the new record the day of Keith's funeral. He would ride around listening to it with tear filled eyes as did an entire nation of country music lovers after hearing the finally perfect, Keith Whitley.

Keith Whitley died May 9, 1989 of alcohol poisoning after a weekend of binge drinking. He left behind a newborn son, Jesse Keith Whitley, and his widow country artist, Lorrie Morgan. He also left behind a huge question. What would Keith Whitley have accomplished had he lived longer? I don't know, but I do know that on May 9, 1989, a new Honky Tonk Angel joined the ranks of millions of others, and I am grateful. "Darling this time, let your memories die, when you hold me tonight, don't close your eyes."

I Swear

For better or worse til death do us part, I'll love you with every beat of my heart. I swear...

Chapter 19

FRANK J. MYERS

Frank J. Myers

GARY BAKER

Gary Baker

I SWEAR

All of the co-writers that I have met and written with came from different places in this country and different walks of life.

Such is the case with the writing team Baker/Myers.

Gary Baker and Frank J. Myers would collaborate on several hit songs, but it was one song that would forever place them in the "I Wish I Had Written That" Hall of Fame.

Frank J. Myers was the son of a fiddle player, Melvin "Pee Wee" Myers, and would learn to play guitar at an early age and never look back. After marrying his wife, Melinda, in 1980 the

"If you confess with your lips that Jesus is Lord and believe in your heart that God raised Him from the dead, you will be saved."
Romans 10:9

Myers' would make the pilgrimage to Nashville the following year.

Frank landed a gig playing guitar for country superstar Eddie Raven and went on to be his road manager as well as a collaborator on several hit songs for Raven including, "I Got Mexico" and "Bayou Boys."

Gary Baker followed his mentor and friend, Lenny LeBlanc, to Muscle Shoals, Alabama and put down roots there. Baker became a part of the country group, The Shooters, that would see some success before disbanding. Following the band break up, Gary soon joined Frank Myers in Marie Osmond's band after Myers left the Eddie Raven band in 1990. It was during this time with Marie Osmond that Gary and Frank would flourish with their songwriting. Their first success showed up in a #1 hit for the group Alabama with "Once In A Lifetime" in 1993.

With a co-write scheduled with legendary hit writer/producer Robert Byrne on the books, Gary called Frank with the idea for a song called, "I Swear." On the three-hour drive to Muscle Shoals, Alabama, Frank worked out what would become the now famous chorus to the song.

Upon arriving to write with Baker and Byrne, Myers was given the idea for a different song that they would all write that morning.

After Robert Byrne had left the co-write, Myers played Gary the chorus to the idea for the song, "I Swear." Loving what he heard, the two of them went over to one of the writing rooms at Fame Studio and wrote the verses for the song.

A demo of the song would soon follow, but that demo

would garnish no hard looksies or chances for a big cut.

Time would go by before one of Marie Osmond's band members would put a track to the song that would better enhance the song's potential.

Honky Tonk Angels and alcohol shouldn't really make a good mix, but in country music the two will eventually get together.

Frank J. Myers lined up a co-write with new Atlantic country artist John Michael Montgomery. He drove to the house of Montgomery in his home state of Kentucky. Soon after getting there he realized that John, his brother Eddie, and friend Troy Gentry (later to be the duo Montgomery/Gentry) were consuming a good amount of Kentucky born and bred Jim Beam whiskey. It was soon obvious that a co-write was not going to happen that day. Instead, Frank took advantage of the opportunity to play the artist some of his songs. When John Michael heard the song "I Swear," he liked it and took a copy of the song. Angels and whiskey may not seem like a Godly thing, but remember that wedding in Cana?

Now the part that I like about the success of this song is that the publishers of this monster hit were not one of the big powerhouse publishing machines in Nashville at the time. Dennis Morgan, writer of such great hits as Ronnie Milksop's "Smokey Mountain Rain," and the timeless hit from Barbara Mandrell, "I Was Country When Country Wasn't Cool," would share the publishing with Frank Myers, and that little house of hits in Muscle Shoals, Alabama, Fame Studios. Rick Hall would own rights to Gary Baker's share.

The song got passed along to John Michael Montgomery's producer, Scott Hendricks, who would eventually cut it on him for the album *Kicking It Up*.

"I Swear" would become a #1 song for John Michael Montgomery and bring the writers a CMA and NSAI Song of the

Year Award and later a Grammy.

Honky Tonk Angels are always staying busy. While the country version of the song was tearing up the charts, Atlantic Records was developing a new pop group, All Four One.

Baker and Myers were called into the office of former A&R head for Atlantic Records Nashville, Al Cooley. Cooley played them a very pop produced version of the song with the new group. That version of "I Swear" would go to #1 on the Pop charts as well.

Honky Tonk Angels took a very different route for this song and its writers. Years later, it's clear to see that they are big fans of love songs as well. You can't make this stuff up, I Swear.

Bernie with Mr. Muscle Shoals, Rick Hall during Country Radio Seminar 2014

Kiss This

She was a woman on a mission.

Here to drown and forget him.

So I set her up again to wash him down...

Chapter 20

Aaron Tippin

Philip Douglas

KISS THIS

To understand country music you have to understand the working man first. Merle Haggard and Johnny Cash, as well as Loretta Lynn, found that singing to that group of listeners was both appealing and profitable. Songs like "The Working Man," "You Ain't Woman Enough To Take My Man," and "One Piece At A Time" were all aimed at middle-class America.

I think it's safe to say that the majority of the record buying public wants to hear someone sing about what it is they

Thea Tippin

117

" In your anger do not sin: and do not let the sun go down while you are still angry."
Ephesians 4:26

are feeling or going through at the time. Sometimes it's a big love song that the women can get all tingly about while dreaming about that kind of love. Other times it's a good old-fashioned drinking song that everyone can relate to on a Friday night. Once in a great while, a song comes along that pushes a different button with its listeners. A song that comes close to going too far but just close enough to get away with it. Songs like Confederate Railroad's "Trashy Women," or Trace Adkins' "Honky Tonk Badonkadonk" are great examples.

Aaron Dupree Tippin was born in Pensacola, Florida in 1958. He learned that singing was something he was not only good at, but also singing for common folks was where his heart was.

By the time he was 20 years old, Aaron had a job flying commercially. That would be a skill that would come in handy later on with the onset of his success as an artist.

In 1986, Aaron made his move to Nashville where he soon competed in the TNN show *You Can Be A Star*. His performance on the show landed him a songwriter deal at the famed Acuff/Rose publishing company. That publishing deal soon landed him cuts with Charlie Pride, David Ball, and Mark Collie.

Like so many songwriters that wish to be major artists, Aaron was playing the songwriter club scene in Nashville. He used to wear this old beat up John Deere ball cap showing his homegrown roots.

One night, he showcased at a live venue directly across the

street from the famous Bluebird Café and was so captivating that he was given his first record deal with RCA.

Aaron released a timely single called "You've Got To Stand For Something" just about the time the first Gulf War started. It became the rallying song for US troops in combat and reached #6 on the country Billboard chart. The other singles off his freshman record would not fair as well.

His second RCA record would garner him a three-week run at the top of the chart with the song "There Ain't Nothin' Wrong With The Radio." He had other hits with similar blue-collar songs like "Working Man's PhD," which he wrote with veteran hit man Philip Douglas.

In 1998, Tippin exited RCA for a new deal on the newly formed Lyric Street Records, a subsidiary of the Walt Disney Company. The first single "For You I Will" wound up at #6 on the charts.

To achieve real greatness, you sometimes have to wait on the Honky Tonk Angels to pay you a visit.

I've said many times that God uses our so-called mistakes to do His works. Sometimes we can say or do something that would seem offensive to God. Words have very little substance with God. What we see as a bad word is to Him only a word. Actions are more important to the Creator of all languages.

Philip Douglas, who had teamed up with Aaron in the past with his hits, "Blue Angel" and "Working Mans PhD," drove from his home in Bowling Green, Kentucky to the Tippin residence in Smithville, Tennessee, which by the way is 100 miles one way. Now that's dedication. Like all successful artists and songwriters in this crazy business, Aaron was blessed with a very talented and hard working partner.

Aaron's wife, Thea, is a Greek as is her name. This is important to know. She landed a job working for Reba McEntire at her new office out by the fairgrounds. Mr. Tippin was recently signed to Reba's management company, so the two of them would soon interact with each other at different functions and well, you know the rest.

The Tippin's knew that they wanted a nice place away from Music Row to raise their family, so they made the move to Smithville, Tennessee, a good forty-five minute drive from Nashville. Now, Thea is Greek. Remember I mentioned that and said it is important. Being Greek, Thea loves to cook. This is where I think that the Honky Tonk Angels got very creative.

So Philip Douglas was on his way to write with Aaron, while Thea was getting unwanted cooking advice from her husband, Aaron. This is not something that I recommend any man do with his wife; especially, if she is Greek, French, Irish, Italian, or just a woman. This unwanted intervention led to Thea telling Aaron that in her mind he was wrong, and that he could kiss her.....well you know.

So when Philip Douglas got there to write, they all jokingly said it would be a fun idea to write a song called "Kiss This."

Aaron and I used to work out together at this crazy little gym right off Music Row, so it came as no surprise that with his success, he would build a gym in his house. The gym is where Philip and Aaron always wrote songs.

Philip had just been complaining to Aaron and Thea that he was tired of all the songs on the radio with the word "kiss" in it, like "This Kiss." So "Kiss This" would be a fun song to write and was never thought to be anything more.

A little over an hour later, Aaron and Philip would be in Tippin's home studio laying down a basic demo of the song.

Doug Howard and Randy Goodman were heading up the new Lyric Street label. When Aaron told his co-writer, Philip Douglas, that he was going to play the new song that came out of a heated tiff with his wife, Thea to the label, and he didn't expect much to come of it. Well, a lot came of it; a platinum record by way of another #1 song for Aaron Tippin.

For the newer songwriters and artists reading this story, it should be noted that sometimes off the wall songs are the ones that go off the charts. People want to hear someone on radio express their own thoughts. To this day, when I am in a club and Aaron's song "Kiss This" comes over the DJ's speakers, it always gets the same response even after all this time. There's just something appealing about getting away with telling someone to kiss your....you know what in a song.

So the next time you get worked up over something, don't be too surprised if those Honky Tonk Angels don't try to convince you to put those words into a song.

Alibis

Alibis and lying eyes and all the best lines Lord knows she's heard them all...

Chapter 21

RANDY BORDEAUX

Randy Boudreaux

ALIBIS

Dictionary.com defines the word "alibi" as an excuse or story used to attempt to avoid blame.

God knows (He really does) that we've all probably tried to do that once or twice in our lifetime. They usually come back, however, to bite us in the butt. The Truth will set you free, so the Bible tells us.

Randy Boudreaux moved to Nashville from Louisiana to become at the very least a songwriter. It wasn't that he didn't know how to write songs; he just didn't know what to do with the ones he had already written.

Success on Music Row can be in one minute as elusive as

"A false witness will not go unpunished, and he who breathes out lies will not escape."
Proverbs 19:5

Bigfoot and then just like that, every door in town swings open for you, and you are on a roll. Randy had landed a job selling copy machines and was not any better at selling them than he was his songs.

After not reaching the sales figures that his company expected, he was let go from his job. Randy told me that he only took the job to pay his bills while he found a way to get his songs recorded. Now he was without a job and still was no closer to getting his songs landed on a major country artist.

Randy's wife told him that he had never really given his heart and desires to God, and that it would never work until he did. Well, that's what Randy did. He got on his knees with his wife that day and gave his life over to God. Ask, Believe, Receive. I know firsthand that that is the only path to true success with God.

After Randy had let it all go and turned his life over to Jesus, he continued looking for work. One day, while filling out a job application, he found the words to "Alibis" filtering into his creativeness. He wrote them on the back of that job application. Now that is faith right there, folks.

"Alibis" would be recorded several times before it would land in the hands of Tracy Lawrence.

Both Joe Diffie and Tracy Byrd recorded the song, but it never found its way to country radio on either one of them.

I think I wrote my first song in the third grade, but it was really a rewrite of the old Barry Sadler song "Ballad of the Green Berets." It got me suspended from Catholic school. Oh, the shame.

Tracy Lawrence, as the story goes, started a tad bit younger at the tender age of four. His mother had to write the lyrics down for him. So it would go to say that songwriting became a passion for Tracy.

Born in Atlanta, Texas and raised in Foreman, Arkansas, Tracy Lawrence learned to perform and sing country music. Now all he needed was a five-hour trip east to Twangtown, USA.

Tracy found his way around the music world that is very much its own institution where you have to study every day to pass, or you will fail. A timely performance at the Bluebird Cafe would align him with a manager named Wayne Edwards who would help him get his break at Atlantic Records.

Here's a side note that proves God has a plan and won't let anything keep it from happening. One night while returning to his manager's hotel room in Nashville, some men attempted to rob Tracy and Wayne. Tracy fought with the men who were armed with a gun and was shot four times before the men ran off. Tracy's wounds were serious but turned out not to be life threatening. Praise God again!

Rick Blackburn ran Atlantic Records back then. He had a unique way of picking singles for his artist. Everyone that worked at the label, from the receptionist to the kid that stacked the boxes of records in the inventory room, had a vote. I think it was one through ten. As a rule, whatever songs scored the most points became a single, and most often a big smash. "Alibis" would go on to be the first hit off the album of the same name. It would also produce a multi-platinum selling record and garnish the 1993 New Male Artist Award for Tracy.

"Alibis" is a song written about someone that is trying to win someone's heart that has gone through a relationship of lies. Although it is about a bad situation, it served a purpose to not just become a huge number one song for both Tracy Lawrence and the writer Randy Boudreaux, but would also be a wake-up call song for countless women and men that were dealing with the decision to remain in a similar relationship.

So many times country music produces thought provoking songs, and often it is for good. Hey, what are the chances that God knew that when he whispered the idea into Randy Boudreaux's ear, while he was filling out a job application for what would have been another dead end job?

God hears our prayers, but how often do we fail to hear Him? When we finally do open up our ears and hearts to His will and His way, doors seem to fly open ever so effortlessly.

Sold

She's got ruby red lips, blonde hair blue eyes and I'm about to bid my heart goodbye...

Chapter 22

Rich Fagen

Robb Royer

SOLD (THE GRUNDY COUNTY AUCTION INCIDENT)

I've heard it said that songs are like old photographs. When you hear them, they take you back to that place when you first heard them. They remind you of those times and things you did back then.

I feel so blessed (my favorite word these days) to look back at the rich history of country music that has been a part of me.

Whenever I hear the song, "Sold, The Grundy County Auction Incident," I am transported back to the old Commodore Lounge at the West End Holiday Inn in Nashville. My friend,

"...and they were selling their possessions and belongings and distributing the proceeds to all."
Acts 2:44:45

Rich Fagan, was fresh off a big hit with John Michael Montgomery with his song, "Be My Baby Tonight," and was playing a round with me there one night.

John Michael Montgomery was on Atlantic Records, and I had been having success there with other artists on their roster.

The head of A&R was a salty character named Al Cooley. Al used to be my song plugger when I was writing at MCA Music, and we had a shared taste in music and bowling. Al was a 300 bowler. We'll get back to Mr. "I Could Have Been a Pro Bowler" in a minute.

Rich was notorious for playing either really clever funny songs, or songs that hit you smack in the heart. On that particular night, Rich did three songs as I recall. He started with his big George Strait cut, "Over Night Male" then played a new song, and finished with his crowd pleasing, would ya could ya "Be My Baby Tonight," John Michael Montgomery. I was really knocked out by the new song. It was a very tongue twisting tune about falling for a girl as if your heart was on the auction block. "She's an eight, she's a nine, she's a ten I know. She's got ruby red lips, blonde hair blue eyes, and I'm about to bid my heart goodbye."

It was one of those songs you wanted to hear again, so you could memorize some of the lyrics to share later with your friends.

Back to Mr. "I Could Have Been a Pro Bowler," Al Cooley. I had a meeting the next day with Al to play him songs for whatever project he was working on that day.

He asked if I had anything for John Michael Montgomery that would be similar to Rich Fagan's smash, "Be My Baby Tonight." I told him no, but I knew who did. I proceeded to try to explain the new song that Rich had played the night before at the Commodore Lounge. Despite my best efforts, I couldn't recall any of the cool, clever lines in the song. I just told Al that he had to hear it.

Rich Fagan told me that he and a former member of the 70's pop band "Bread," Robb Royer, were at a benefit one night where they were auctioning off signed musical things. Robb thought the idea of writing an auctioneer song was long over-due.

In the process of writing the song, Rich Fagan remembered a line from a musical show that used to be held at several of the local venues called the Chili Shack Show. It was a collection of songs and improv sets. In one of the shows, the main character, Austin Church, was auctioning off a trip to beautiful Grundy County, Tennessee (God was sewing seeds long in advance).

Now, again, you can call it coincidence that they were there at an event that had an auction going on, and that it made them think about writing a song about auctioning off your heart to some girl, but I am pretty sure that the whole thing was worked out long in advance by The Big Guy.

I'm also not sure if Al Cooley reached out to Rich Fagan about the clever song that I had told him that I had heard, but I do know that John Michael Montgomery recorded it on his self-titled CD in 1995. It would be his second #1 off the record and go on to be the 1995 Billboard Single of the Year.

Years later, I am profoundly aware of the impact that songs have on so many people that we as writers don't even take into consideration when we write them.

John Michael Montgomery would go on to an even bigger platform as an artist. That meant that his band members would be making more money than I'm sure they needed. You can even take it to the extreme and say that local and touring bands would learn the song, and it would enhance their live shows in nightclubs around the country. So many lives changed all because God thought that two talented songwriters should attend a benefit that auctioned off things to raise money, and leave them with the idea for a clever song. I don't know if you're convinced yet but as for me, I am definitely "Sold" on the idea.

When She Cries

When she cries at night and she
doesn't think that I can hear her...

Chapter 23

MARC BEESON
Marc Beeson

SONNY LEMAIRE
Sonny LeMaire

WHEN SHE CRIES

Writing a song about how it affects you when the woman you love cries is not a cookie cutter idea for most of the songwriters on the streets of Music Row. I don't think that writing a song about it was actually on the minds of the writers of the song "When She Cries" the day they wrote it.

I met Marc Beeson shortly after he got to Nashville from L.A. I had a duplex off Belmont Boulevard not far from The Row. I think we met at EMI just hanging around together.

I know that I had not heard him sing until we sat down at my place to write for the first time. Marc is a melody magnet to

135

"Hear Oh Lord when I
cry with my voice, and
be gracious to me and
answer me"
Psalm 27:2

say the least. He had so many different melodies coming at me that I didn't know which one to latch onto first. I remember thinking, "This guy is gonna get a record deal; he is so pop sounding," and that's the direction Nashville was leaning towards in the early 90's.

Marc and I would not only go on to be good at writing together but also great friends. We used to hang out in the lobby of EMI waiting for Mark Bright, producer for Blackhawk, Rascal Flatts, and Carrie Underwood to name a few, to come out of his office so we could hit him up for a free lunch courtesy of EMI. Mark was the head song plugger at EMI before he started producing major acts on radio. Marc and I were both a couple of freeloaders when it came to lunch back then.

Marc's first cut in Nashville came as no surprise from a pop act, Exile, with the song "Even Now." Marc met Exile bass player and an all around great guy, Sonny LeMaire, in the studio while the band was recording his song. The two decided to try to write one day and see what fell out.

The group, Exile, originated out of Lexington, Kentucky. You know, all the pop acts come from there. Yeah right.

The voices of J.P. Pennington, Les Taylor, and Sonny LeMaire will forever be heard on classic rock radio. Songs like "Kiss You All Over," "Woke Up In Love," and "I Can't Get Close Enough" were required songs on my old band's set list for wherever we played back then.

Like me, Marc Beeson was more than familiar with the band Exile, so getting his first cut on them had to be a bit of a confidence booster for the new kid on The Row.

Marc says that the day they wrote "When She Cries," they were working off of a melody that he (remember the melody magnet) had been kicking around for awhile.

When you write with Marc, he kind of hums what sounds like words, but he doesn't really hear anything he says. Whatever he was humming to both of them at some point sounded like, "When she cries at night..."

If you were to ask most of the writers of the greatest songs ever, the majority would tell you that the song pretty much wrote itself, hello? Honky Tonk Angels me thinks.

When Michelangelo was asked how he created such amazing statues, he said that the statues were always there, and that he simply chiseled away the stone until they appeared. I think songs are like that too.

I think God wrote them already and just sits around waiting for us to show up to let them out of His storage vault or wherever He keeps them.

So Sonny and Marc wrote a very powerful song about a man's spouse, and the hurt she sometimes feels with a really catchy chorus. Now, what?

Marc would have loved to have gotten another cut on Exile, but they were not in the recording mode at that time. Marc was trying to get a record deal as an artist himself, but that was not on the table at the time. So Marc turned the song over to his trusted friends at EMI Publishing to see what they could do with it.

EMI was located in what used to be the old Combine Publishing office at 35 Music Sq. East. It was an easy walk to the RCA Records office back then. We used to go over to RCA with a group of writers and solely played songs on the guitars. That was pretty cool back then.

The group, Restless Heart, was smack dab in the middle of a serious reconstruction phase. Lead singer Larry Stewart had decided to venture out on his own as a solo artist and left the band. The former drummer of the band, John Dittrich, would fill that void. When Marc got the news that the band was looking to record his song, but that lead singer Larry Stewart wasn't in the band anymore, one would think that Marc would have been disappointed. But the way Marc saw it was that he hadn't had enough cuts yet not to get excited about any of them.

I had a 1989 Chevrolet truck. It was actually required that all successful songwriters have a truck, and Marc let me hear the cut, so we sat in my truck and cranked it up.

Marc asked me if I thought it was too pop. I said, "Heck yeah, pop enough to cross over into the pop charts."

Tears have been a very successful subject matter in country music over the years. I don't think many of those songs touch the hearts of so many the way that "When She Cries" does still to this day.

God is moved by tears. John 11:33, "When Jesus saw her weeping … he was deeply moved and troubled." It comes as no surprise that He would send His Holy angels to open His vault and pour out the words that He had stored away for such a song.

Restless Heart released "When She Cries" in August of 1992. It reached #9 on the Country Billboard chart and would also cross over into the Billboard Top 100 chart reaching the #11 position. It would also get a Grammy nomination for Best Country Group Performance.

Not a bad day's work for a new kid in town and a veteran pop songwriter. Sometimes it's a good idea to simply open up your heart and see what falls out.

Here in the Real World

Cowboys don't cry and heroes don't die. Good always wins again and again...

Chapter 24

Alan Jackson

Mark Irwin

HERE IN THE REAL WORLD

What does a kid from the Bronx, a cowboy from Georgia, a businessman from Australia, and an accountant from Texas have in common?

The first time I met Mark Irwin, I was in the mood for a cup of coffee while playing the Bluebird Cafe here in Nashville. Songwriter nights at the Bluebird were relatively new there and resembled the Wild West as far as political correctness went. Smoking was still permitted, and only the cream of the crop was allowed to play. Mark Irwin had just arrived in town and within a week, landed a job as a bar back at the soon to become World Famous Bluebird Cafe.

"As He is, so are we in this world"
1 John 4:17

I was well into my third single on the radio, and was recently allowed into the realm of the boys club at the Bluebird thanks to Don Schlitz, who was brave enough to let me open for him a few times.

That night, I was playing a round with my hero/pal Russell Smith of Amazing Rhythm Aces fame.

So off to the bar for a coffee I went. I didn't know Mark until it was time to play the round, but I was greeted with a smile and a very bad cup of coffee.

At the time, there was a waitress, who worked there and was a fan of the new bartender's songwriting talents. She asked me, rather told me that I was going to write with Mark Irwin, and we would do great together. One, I was on a roll as a successful country songwriter and two, Mark Irwin was from the Bronx, New York. What the heck was she thinking trying to get me to write with a rookie and a kid from the Bronx? What the heck would a guy from there have to do with country music?

But Debra McEuen, aka "Stretch," the waitress was not the kind of girl you said no to.

Mark Irwin moved to Nashville at the perfect time to jump into the songwriting world. The late 80's was a window when country artists were emerging quicker than buds on an early March Bradford Pear tree in Twangtown. A steady stream of artists were taking off. Joe Diffie, Ricky Van Shelton, Mark Chestnut, and King George Strait were running up and down the Billboard charts.

Mark visited the Nashville Songwriters International Association his first few days in town and met with President Richard Helms. Helms suggested that they go to the Bluebird to see a writer named J. Fred Knobloch. While listening to Knobloch, he overheard one of the waitresses mention that they were in need of a bar back. Mark started working the next day. Honky Tonk Angels?

Mark and I surprisingly wrote really great together, but also became really good friends.

He found his way into the office of a brand new publishing company that was run by a guy from Australia. Barry Coburn and his wife, Jewel, started 1010 Music, which was located at … duh, 1010 Sixteen Ave South. Barry was managing a new kid named Alan Jackson. Alan was working at the now defunct Nashville Network in the mailroom. Barry put his new writer from the Bronx and a long legged Georgia kid together for a co-write. Mark says the co-write didn't last over two hours. He said that Alan had a couple of lines but no title or melody. "Cowboys don't lie, and heroes don't die." Well heck, that sounds like the makings of a good country song, thought Mark. The song was written like so many classics are in less than an hour. They put it down on a cassette and made plans to get together again soon.

Nashville's record labels have a tendency to reject artists the first time around. Artists like Kenny Chesney, Garth Brooks, and Blake Shelton were all turned down by every label in town. So went the struggle for Barry Coburn while trying to find a home for Alan Jackson. After showcases and meetings with all the big labels, Barry was at a stand still on his search for Alan.

Enter Honky Tonk Angels again. Mega record mogul Clive Davis was heading up Arista Records with such huge artists as Barry Manilow, and Aerosmith. The record sales were just taking off in the mid 80's for country artists, so it was an appealing prospect for Mr. Davis.

He opened the Arista label just off of Music Row in 1989. He brought in hit songwriter Tim DuBois to head it up. As luck would have it, they were looking for a good-looking hat act. Voila, Honky Tonk Angels at their best. Barry Coburn was soon Arista Records' new best friend. Alan Jackson was signed to the label with the help of Glen Campbell in 1989. His first single, "Blue Blooded Woman" would not break the Top 40 on the Billboard charts.

Tim DuBois was in need of a country smash. What he wasn't counting on was what would become a country music standard. He and Alan were going over song pitches and songs that Alan hadn't played the label yet. Tim wanted to hear everything Alan had. "Here In The Real World" wasn't a song that Alan was totally comfortable with singing, so it was not on his A list.

After hearing the song, Tim DuBois was certain that he had heard Alan Jackson's first big hit. It would reach #3 on the charts, and be the title track for an album that would produce three more monster hits, "Wanted," "Chasing That Neon Rainbow," and "I'd Love You All Over Again."

So the fact that a kid from the Bronx would get a job at the biggest writer's venue in Nashville his first week in town, sign a writer's deal with a new publisher from Australia who had just signed a brand new artist to manage, put them together to write, plus the fact that a big shot in the music world, Clive Davis, would start a new country label up just as Alan Jackson was looking for a record label, proves that there most definitely are Honky Tonk Angels "Here In the Real World."

There's a Girl in Texas

There's a girl in Texas ,there's a girl in Texas that does...

Chapter 25

Trace Adkins

Vip Vipperman

THERE'S A GIRL IN TEXAS

It's hard enough to get your foot in the door at a major re-cord label. So when the head of that label asks you to write a specific song to impress him, you had better nail it down pretty good.

Trace Adkins was building barns for a living and playing when he could at a local bar in Nashville when I first heard his name.

My song plugger back then was Micki Foster. She is the daughter of the legendary songwriter and producer, Fred Foster "Me and Bobby McGee."

Micki had played a song of mine, "I Can Only Love You Like

"Then this is what he said, I will tear down my barns and build bigger ones and there I will store my surplus."
Luke 12:18

A Man," for Blake Mevis "If You're Looking For A Stranger," George Strait. Mevis asked if he could have the song for a new artist he was working with, Trace Adkins. At first, Blake shopped Trace to Atlantic Records but never got the deal there to happen. Mevis told me some time ago that when Scott Hendricks, the head of Capitol Records back then, heard Trace sing the song "I Can Only Love You Like A Man," he was excited about finding more songs for him and decided to sign him to the label at Capitol Records.

So there was that big foot of Trace's in the door at Capitol Records. All that was needed were a few big hit songs to record.

Ten years earlier, another new artist looking for a few hit songs found his first from a song written by Buddy Blackman and Vip Vipperman. That song was "1982," Randy Travis's first big hit off the "Storms of Life" record. It's funny how time flies in Nashville. So many new artists arrive every day looking for their chance to prove they have what it takes to make it in Twangville. Ten years would pass, and Vip would again be asked to take a chance on a brand spanking new artist with one of his works.

Blake Mevis decided to put Vip Vipperman together with his new artist to try to write a few songs for the possible impending record project on Trace Adkins.

Now, like I said, Trace was building barns at the time, and nothing creates creativity like working with your hands. I have no doubt that God puts the creative souls He loves into those jobs for just that reason.

So Trace and his new label head needed songs, and Trace had just moved to Nashville in 1994 from Texas. Scott Hendricks asked Trace if there was a girl back there in Texas that he had left behind.

"Well, of course, there is," responded Trace. "There's always a girl."

So with a Tom Petty feel on the guitar, hit songwriter Vip Vipperman, and soon-to-be Country Music Icon. Trace Adkins, set out to write a song about leaving a girl in Texas for a life in Tennessee. Simple plan, huh?

Do you suppose that God had anything to do with Trace moving from Springhill, Louisiana to Texas, so that there would be a "girl in Texas?" Or that He might get his angels to work on what it was that Trace needed to write about from the mind of Scott Hendricks? Add in the chances that the writer of Randy Travis' "1982" would be brought into the mix with the help of producer Blake Mevis. Blake, who by the way already knew a thing or two about country singers from Texas as he was the original producer for country king George Strait with hits like "Unwound."

"There's A Girl In Texas" would like so many great songs take a few rewrites and edits to get it to where it needed to be. Once it was finished, it got a looksie from other artists. Even Ronnie Dunn of Brooks and Dunn wanted to record it.

It went on to be Trace's first single. It would end up in the Top 20 on the famed Billboard charts and be the catalyst for Trace's *Dreamin Out Loud* record, which would have three other hits, including "Every Light In The House Is On."

I look back now and what seemed like randomness and circumstance, I see now that it was clearly a well planned out execution of God's work.

I'm glad that I took a chance on this new artist that was building barns for a living at the time. I'm also very glad that there was, "A Girl In Texas."

Riding With
Private Malone

And though you may take her and make her your own, you'll always be riding with Private Malone...

Chapter 26

Thom Shepherd

Wood Newton

RIDING WITH PRIVATE MALONE

According to the November 1965 issue of Car and Driver magazine, the new 1966 Corvette Stingray was going to be coming out with a few more horses under the hood than the 1965 model. To a young man with very few speed laws and lots of old back roads just waiting to be raced on, this was a dream come true. Chevrolet would do away with the 396 cubic inch engine for a beefier 427 that would make putting your foot on the gas pedal a whole new adventure.

The War in Vietnam or the Conflict In Southeast Asia as

the White House liked to call it, was really ramping up at the beginning of 1966. If you were of draft age, there was a good chance that Uncle Sam was going to disrupt your summer plans after high school graduation. The number of young men selected by the government in a lottery draft had jumped from about 84,000 in 1965 to over 382,000 in 1966. The casualty rate was climbing with every new battle over there.

If I were a young man fresh out of high school knowing that I had to report to basic training with the prospects of being sent to Vietnam to fight, I would spend every dime I had to buy my dream car just in case I didn't make it back.

Wood Newton was getting big cuts in Nashville, while I was still trying to figure out which bars not to play in out in Wyoming in the early 80's. Believe me there were a few. The first time his name showed up on my radar was the big Oak Ridge Boys smash, "Bobbie Sue," and then again with Steve Wariner with "It's What I Didn't Do." When I got to meet him a few years later, I was glad to find that the man behind those songs was such a likable person. Over my ten year run at EMI Publishing, Wood and I would crank out a few good ones now and then. He recently told me the story about his friend Jeff Bateson, "The Rock," for Tracy Lawrence doing a round at the old After the Opry Spotlight Show with Mathew Gillon. The show was always live on 650 WSM. The studio was inside the luxurious Opryland Hotel on the first floor by the main lobby. Speakers were set up outside in the corridor, so that the people walking by could see and hear the show. This one particular evening, Jeff Batson was doing a round with a fellow Show Me State writer, Thom Shepherd. Wood felt after hearing Mr. Shepherd's songs, that the two of them might be able to write well together. So Wood got the number for the young man from the St. Louis area.

After the two of them had sat down to write, Thom brought

out an idea about a story he had read. Someone had purchased a 1960's car and found out that the car would always be playing an Oldies station when it was started up (enter eerie organ music). Well, they kicked the idea around and came up with a story line for the song. A young man would leave his car behind and be killed in Vietnam, and then have the car be bought by someone to drive around years later.

After a couple writing sessions, they started to fine-tune the song a bit. What year and make should the car be? Wood still had a library card to the Green Hills Library, so off they went. Note that this was a few years before Wikipedia and Google, so that was a great source of information back then and by the way, still is. Wood had always had visions of owning a 1966 Corvette. They researched it, and it was called strangely "The Dream Car." Now all they needed was a little more storyline, and they would have it wrapped up.

Wood was producing a new artist, David Ball, for Dualtone Records, and his record was basically finished. Wood played the song for David, but it didn't quite resonate with him until he heard it sung at a songwriter night by Thom Shepherd. They went in and recorded a version of the song but felt that it didn't belong on the record that was mostly wrapped up.

The song would make the new record and be released as a single in August of 2001. I'm pretty sure that everyone is aware of what happened on September 11, 2001 as it is well documented and will never be forgotten.

The song was just getting going up the charts when the planes flew into those twin towers in Manhattan. Patriotism probably played a big role in the success of the song.

There is nothing like having a song about American soldiers on the charts at the right time.

Wood tells the story of how years later, while working with the Nashville Songwriters Association International, he was in

Washington DC. The group visited the Vietnam Wall and found lots of young Irishmen named Malone that had paid the ultimate sacrifice in Vietnam. Thom Shepherd says that the reason they chose that name for the song was that the name Malone rhymed with the word "Home."

There would be no Andrew Malone on the wall, but it was still a hard reality check for Wood Newton to ironically see the name Malone on the wall so many times. All too often, we as songwriters create a story in a song that later appears to be about a real person and a real situation. I guess that's why the best songs are so successful, but it doesn't take away the agony of feeling connected to those that were in real life and living out those stories.

The song talks about the man that goes to buy what is advertised as a '66 Chevrolet for sale for a thousand dollars only to find his dream car in an old barn. Later in the song, a letter is found in the glove box written by a young man that went off to defend his country. He states that whoever finds this note now owns his car, and hopes they enjoy it as much as he did. Powerful imagery and timely delivery by a new artist on the country music charts. The song talks about both the periodic visions of what looks like a soldier riding shotgun in the Corvette, and the thought that a soldier pulled the driver out of a fiery crash that destroyed the car.

Angels? Well heck yeah. If I didn't believe in them, this book wouldn't be in your hands. Do I believe the story could be true? Yes, but more importantly, I believe that long before any of the Malone's shipped off to Southeast Asia to never return, God was fully aware that a song bearing the name Private Andrew Malone would reach #2 on the Country charts for David Ball. He also knew about 9/11, and the mood that the country would be in after that horrific day. I believe that Wood Newton and Thom Shepherd were not sitting in a room with the ghost of a soldier the day they started the song, but with caring angels, who wanted to help bring about a song, and would be needed to bind a nation and heal wounds from a war that was never a popular one. "….I thank God I was riding with Private Malone."

Bernie with Thom Shepherd

155

I Don't Need Your
Rocking Chair

My bodies old but it ain't impaired.

Well I don't need your rocking chair...

Chapter 27

Billy Yates

Frank Dycus

I DON'T NEED YOUR ROCKING CHAIR

Ain't it amazing what a six-month beautician's license can get you when God has a mind to make things happen?

I caught up with my old friend Billy Yates to ask him about his first big cut, and I mean a doozy, "I Don't Need Your Rocking Chair," with the great one, George Jones.

I know so many parts and pieces of these stories due to the fact that I have been blessed to be

Kerry Kurt Phillips

"Is not wisdom found among the aged, does not long life bring understanding?"
Job 12:12

around when they happened here in Nashville. However, there are pieces to the puzzle that I never was aware of in so many of these songs until I started this book.

Billy Yates, like me, came to Nashville with the idea of being a country artist, and songwriting was a secondary consideration.

A good songwriter is also a smart businessman. Billy had taken six months to acquire a beautician's license, while still living in his home state of Missouri just in case the whole country superstar thing didn't work out as quickly as he would have liked.

Billy found a great spot to cut hair in a salon on 17th Avenue and as you would imagine, Music Row folks frequented the place now and then.

Anyone who has spent as little as a couple months here knows that everybody knows somebody, who knows somebody in this town.

Billy Yates has a natural country vocal, so he soon found himself with a writing deal at HoriPro, a publishing company just off Music Row. It was one of the last "Good Ol' Boys" writing houses. He was also getting writing sessions with seasoned veteran Frank Dycus, "Marina Del Rey," George Strait. On one of those writing sessions, he met and wrote with Bruce Bouton. Besides being a great songwriter, he is also a world-class steel guitar player and plays in a band with Garth Brooks. They were working on a song called "Walls Can Fall," and Bruce had the melody going in one direction, but Frank Dycus was hearing it more along the lines of a classic George Jones feel. Once they all agreed on the direction, they finished the song soon after.

Billy Yates has a natural gift to be able to put music to words, or something a lot of writers cannot do.

Frank Dycus, shortly after the "Walls Can Fall" co-write, gave his new friend and co-writer Billy Yates a call about a song idea he had.... Now hold that thought for a minute.

 One of the main reasons for my writing this book is to solidify and back up my belief that God knows long in advance what the outcome will be on songs. He will sometimes put what at the time looks like a bad thing in our path to get us to the good thing He has in store for us.

George Jones had turned out a number of very successful records while at Epic CBS. However, the music scene was changing, and the more hardcore country artists were finding it harder and harder to get airplay on the country radio stations that once were so glad to play them.

The duet "Rockin Years" had originally been planned as a duet project with Mr. Jones and Dolly Parton. The label changed their minds and went with the new rising star and ACM Entertainer of the Year, Ricky Van Shelton, to be Dolly's partner on the project. That was a devastating blow to Jones, and he decided to leave the record label after years of hits with them. He found a new home at MCA Records with the label head Tony Brown, whose head of A&R was Renee Bell.

Tony was gathering songs for the project and looking for that comeback hit.

Ok, let's go back to Frank Dycus calling Billy Yates to come write a smash song for George Jones.

Nowadays, it's hard to talk writers into dropping what they are doing when a veteran songwriter says, "Get over here, I've got a hit we need to write." For whatever reason, Billy did cancel his plans, and met with Dycus and another hit songwriter,

Kerry Kurt Phillips, "Almost Home," Craig Morgan.

When Dycus came up with the idea of "I Don't Need Your Rocking Chair," he was aware of the feelings that George Jones had about being bumped off the "Rockin Years" project. Billy's idea was that Mr. Jones would see it as a way to thumb his nose at his former record label if it was a big hit and say, "I Don't Need Your Rockin Years," more or less. Billy knew about these feelings because he was cutting Nancy's—Mr. Jones' wife's—hair, and people do tend to talk when they get in a barbershop chair.

The three wrote the song very quickly and laid down a very rough work tape on a cassette recorder. That version was immediately put in front of the aforementioned, Renee Bell. She put the song on hold and sent it out to Jones to hear overnight.

Billy Yates was at his publishing company, HoriPro, when he was told he had a phone call. He picked up the phone to find none other than George Jones himself on the other end of the line.

George told him that he was going to cut the song later that week on a Wednesday. Needless to say, young Mr. Yates didn't get much sleep that Tuesday night.

Wednesday rolled around and Billy found out where they were cutting the song but Emory Gordy, the Producer, was a pretty big stickler for no outsiders allowed in the session.

Billy drove around to the back door of the studio and waited to see if anyone he knew came in or out. To his surprise, there was George standing at the back door. He introduced himself to Jones and asked if they were going to cut the song that day. George said they would but not until the six o'clock session.

Billy came back right before six and waited until someone went into the studio. When someone did, Billy walked in like he owned the place. He sat down, and no one seemed to notice him. Emory asked George if he was ready to cut "Rockin

Chair." After the band made a few changes to the original work tape production, they cut the song.

Getting a George Jones cut is a huge thing, but this song was special to Jones and would soon get even more personal.

Nancy Jones has a big mind for business, and thought that some of the younger more traditional country artists might want to lend their vocals to the song. The label balked at the idea probably over logistics and costs, but Nancy made some calls and soon the artists were lining up to add their vocals to the track. Vince Gill, Travis Tritt, Clint Black, Mark Chestnutt, Joe Diffie, Patty Loveless, T. Graham Brown, and Pam Tillis all showed up to record vocals and a video of the event. One particular artist that really wanted to be on the session was busy. It was the week of CMA then called "Fan Fair." Garth Brooks had spent the previous entire 24 hours signing autographs without even a bathroom break. He showed up the next morning without going to bed and asked the studio engineer to fire up the track, so he could sing on the song. I love the outpouring that came from the true country artists on this song.

Songs do have their own set of wings. I believe that with all my heart. They find their way despite the obstacles they must overcome. God sent His angels to set in motion a chain of events that would make the idea of writing a song called "I Don't Need Your Rocking Chair" appealing to Billy Yates. It was appealing because he had the inside view point of a legendary country artist because he spent six months learning to cut hair before he moved to Nashville and ended up cutting the hair of George Jones' wife, Nancy.

Mr. Jones would face yet another obstacle. Country radio, despite the mega stars that were now attached to the song, was not going to give it much of a chance. Nancy called Billy Yates to let him know that the song was about to lose momentum at #55 on the Billboard chart. Billy mentioned that he had a list of radio stations that reported to Billboard, and maybe they should try calling them.

So Billy Yates and Nancy Jones set out calling all the radio stations they could. When a radio station programmer would say regretfully they were not going to continue playing the song, the two would put George himself on the phone. I'm guessing It's hard to tell a country legend "no."

The song eventually did stop at the #22 position, but not before the whole world got to see the momentum behind it. "I Don't Need Your Rocking Chair" would go on to be the CMA Event Song of the Year.

Mr. Jones passed away a few years ago, but he left behind a legacy that will never be forgotten; one that proves that the great artists are great because of their knowledge of what their fans want to hear. Billy Yates, Frank Dycus, and Kerry Kurt Phillips wrote a song for George Jones one day, and the Honky Tonk Angels made sure that it found its rightful place in country music history.

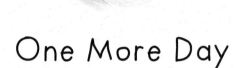

One More Day

One more day one more time one
more sunset and I'd be satisfied. But
even then I know what it would do.
It'd leave me wishing still for one more
day with you...

Chapter 28

Bobby Tomberlin

Steven Dale Jones

ONE MORE DAY

Ok, since you have read this far, I am asking you to take a visual journey with me. Imagine in your mind being the only inhabitants on earth—the first human creations of God. Your life is amazing. You are happy. There is no sorrow, no pain, no guilt, no hatred, and no sin.

Then one day, you totally screw up. You give in to temptation and do the one thing that God has forbidden you to do, and your world is forever changed. Shame, guilt, and fear are what lie before you. Twenty-four hours earlier you were totally in paradise with not a care in the world. Now it's dark, cold, you are scared and for the first time, you realize that you are naked and ashamed.

"Do not boast about tomorrow, for you do not know what the day may bring."
Proverbs 27:1

Don't you believe the thought that crossed Adam and Eve's minds was what they wouldn't do to have a do over? One more chance, one more "it's ok" from God, and just one more day in paradise.

Oh, the countless times I have wished for one more day for many things that I have missed and lost over the years.

Steve Dale Jones and Bobby Tomberlin figured that out way back in 1998 when they sat down to write a new song by the same name. "One More Day" would become the song that the broken hearted would find as their new anthem. With the untimely death of NASCAR legend, Dale Earnhardt, it would also be the song that his fans would request to hear on radio to show their loss for Mr. Earnhardt.

It would all begin when Bobby mentioned the idea to his friend and co-writer, Steven Dale Jones, who had been writing for the famed Rick Hall and Fame Studios in Muscle Shoals, Alabama when they first met. Bobby was working as a DJ at a local radio station, and they spent many a co-write in the hallowed halls of Fame Studios.

However, the writing session's location would play a pivotal role in both the sound of the song and its familiar melody. This sound would catch the ears of both record label powers and the famous country music group, Diamond Rio.

Steven Dale Jones had left Fame Studios and was now relocated to Nashville and was signed to Island Bound Music on 17th Avenue.

Now, I am not saying that fires are a good thing, or that honky tonk angels are pyromaniacs, but I am certain that they may very well have had a hand in starting the fire that burned a good portion of the building Island Bound Music was in shortly before the day that Steven and Bobby sat down to write the song.

One of the song pluggers, whose name shall go unmentioned because we love her, had left a candle burning causing a fire that did extensive damage to the building.

While that building was being restored, the offices were temporarily moved to different quarters.

Steven Dale Jones told me that as a rule, he mostly writes on guitar but when Bobby came in with the melody for this new song, he was reminded of a piano piece that he had learned but could never find a song that it seemed to fit.

"I only knew this one piano piece, and it had to be in the key of C," said Steven.

The temporary office housed the piano of Hall of Famer, Roger Cook, George Strait, "I Just Want To Dance With You."

Steven Dale suggested to Bobby that they try out the melody on Roger's piano.

Like so many of the iconic songs in this book, I remember very well the first time I heard it. The piano played a huge role in its sound and captivating melody.

Once written, Julie Daniels, who ran Island Bound back then, set out pitching the song to artists. Steven Dale told me that he wished they would have taken the time to go in and track a full band demo of the new song. Julie Daniels was confident, however, with the rough work-tape version.

It was grabbed up fairly quickly by the head of A&R for Arista Records, Steve Williams, and the overall thought was that it was a Diamond Rio smash.

That was in late 1998. The song would be recorded in 1999 by the group but would not see radio spins until well into the year 2000. I Guess they were waiting to see if the whole Armageddon thing was real.

As for the path the song took after being recorded, it was Diamond Rio's title track and would eventually become the second single off the record. The group would play the Grand Ole Opry a number of times with the release of the new record but hadn't performed "One More Day" there yet.

Joe Galante had taken over the head position of the record label and was in San Diego where the label execs were meeting to decide the next direction for Diamond Rio. Deb Markland, whose husband Steve worked for the label at the time, was also at the meeting and passed a note to Galante to play the group the song "One More Day." Joe did, and the room was moved to say the least, and agreed it would be the next single.

The song would be a #1 for the group, and the video would touch millions of hearts. Over the years, Bobby and Steven Dale have been approached by hundreds of people that wanted to share their stories about how the song touched them in some kind of manner.

God gives us our days but never promises that we will live to the end of it.. We all make mistakes and seek to find His forgiveness. I am ever so thankful for all of the do-overs that God has given me and for all the "One More Days."

Five O'Clock
Somewhere

Pour me something tall and strong.
Make it a "Hurricane" before I go
insane...

Chapter 29

Don Rollins

Jim Moose Brown

FIVE O'CLOCK
SOMEWHERE

Randy Hardison, cuts with Garth Brooks and Tracy Byrd, would probably have gone on to be a very successful hit songwriter, but died way too young. Very few writers would be so loved in their short time here in this world. Hardison, after meeting Jim Brown for a co-write for some reason immediately said,

"I'm gonna call you Moose," and that was it. Jim Brown would forever after be known as Moose Brown.

Jim "Moose" Brown was born in Dearborn, Michigan but moved to Jonesboro, Arkansas when he was 14 years old. He married his young bride, Jaime, right out of high school and

"These men are not drunk as ye suppose, for it is only the third hour of the day"
Acts 2:15

soon after the honeymoon, they packed up all their stuff and pointed their wheels east toward Nashville.

Moose soon found himself on the road touring with artists like Jim Ed Brown, Bill Anderson, Marie Osmond, and Dan Seals. After being asked to play on a few sessions, he eventually settled into the demo session world as a piano player. Writing songs was not something that really was on his radar for quite a while. Moose was well liked and had moved from only demo recordings to playing on master sessions for major artists. He played on many #1 recordings for artists such as Brad Paisley, Trace Adkins, Hank Williams Jr., and Blake Shelton. He went on to win Keyboard Player of the year multiple years with the Country Music Association.

Fast forward to the early months of 2003, Moose had been co-writing with Don Rollins, and one day after kicking a few other ideas for a song around, Don suggested that they write a song called, "It's Five O'Clock Somewhere." Moose said that he had heard people say that before but had never heard it in a song. From the start, Don had always envisioned the tune with a Jimmy Buffet feel, aka "Margaritaville." Somewhere he had seen a bumper sticker that asked the question, "What Would Jimmy Buffet Do?" With all that input on the table, all that was needed was a catchy melody from Mr. Keyboard Player of the Year.

Now I'm not saying that God wants us all sitting around watching our watches for Happy Hour, but I'm pretty sure that He enjoys a good time just as much as all of Alan Jackson and Jimmy Buffet's fans do.

There is no tried and true method for ensuring a hit song when trying to write one. So many elements have to line up just to get the song recorded, let alone to go on to be big enough to win CMA Song of the Year and a Grammy for Country Event Song of the Year. That said, "Five O'Clock Somewhere" would not only have all those elements lined up, but they would happen at the speed of, well, God.

Don Rollins and Moose Brown wrote the song in early February 2003. They would demo it in March of 2003. They were sure that a new artist, Colt Prather signed to Sony Records, would want the song after hearing he was looking for beach type songs. However, his producer didn't feel it was what they were looking for at the time.

Moose was signed to Seagayle Music, a small publishing company attached to a monster publisher, EMI Music. Again, the perfect storm has to come into play to get a song to the right place at the right time or clever Honky Tonk Angels. What Moose and Don didn't know was that Alan Jackson had been looking for a song that he could record with his long-time hero, Jimmy Buffett.

God knows where those songs are going long before they are even written. I love that about Him.

EMI Music was headed up in 2003 by Gary Overton. A weekly listening session usually took place at EMI first thing on Monday mornings. The song pluggers would take a few hours early in a day and listen to songs that had been recently recorded.

After hearing the song "Five O'Clock Somewhere," Moose Brown got a call from EMI head, Gary Overton. He told Moose that he was having dinner with Alan Jackson. Gary used to manage Alan Jackson. He also told Moose that not only was he going to play it for Alan, but that Mr. Jackson would record it and it would go on to be a huge hit. That's kind of like Babe

Ruth pointing to the left field bleachers and claiming that the next pitch was going over that fence without any doubt.

Well, Gary Overton had been around great songs long enough to know a hit when he heard it, but that was still a pretty bold statement.

Gary Overton may not be able to hit a ball over the left field fence at Fenway Park, but he sure enough was right about his thoughts on "Five O' Clock Somewhere."

Click, click, click, click. The pieces were falling into place at a very rapid pace

Alan was hopeful after hearing the song that they could get Mr. Buffett on board. Once he was, the mega-hit was cast in stone.

The song was recorded in April of 2003 and would hit radio like a tidal wave of big time fun that was long overdue. Country legend Alan Jackson and superstar Jimmy Buffett worked together on a song that promotes having a drink just about any time because it's always "Five O' Clock Somewhere."

Add to that the rare chance that Alan was not scheduled to perform anywhere the night that Buffett wanted to debut the song to his live audience. With video cameras rolling, Buffett and Jackson would record the Event Song of the Year.

I don't know if God is a big lover of beach songs, but He does like us to have a good time now and then so much that he sent his timely angels to open a lot of big doors in a very short period of time, leading me to believe that there are Honky Tonk Angels all around us, and that it's always "Five O'Clock Somewhere."

Friends in
Low Places

Blame it all on my roots,
I showed up in boots,
and ruined your black tie affair...

Chapter 30

Dewayne Blackwell

Earl Bud Lee

FRIENDS IN LOW PLACES

❝ I've got friends in low places. Where the whiskey drowns and the beer chases my blues away, but I'll be ok...."

I was in the tiny town of Birr, Ireland doing a show at a local pub there the winter of 2015. My guitar player, Simon Brady, in addition to being an amazing guitar and mandolin player, was a walking jukebox. This guy could play hundreds of songs from Sinatra to Cash, and he played all the guitar parts just like the record. While I was taking a break and letting Simon entertain the incredibly enthusiastic crowd for a few songs, I was approached by a young man by the bar. He had Down's Syndrome, was wearing a cowboy hat, and he asked me if I could please play some Garth Brooks music. I told him that I didn't play any but that maybe my friend Simon, the human jukebox, could.

It took only the opening seventeen words of the song to turn the place upside down. "Blame it all on my roots, I showed up in boots, and spoiled your black tie affair."

Garth Brooks had played Ireland back in 1994 and was hugely successful, but I was really blown away by the response from the crowd that night at the rowdy little pub in Birr, Ireland some 21 years later.

So, you have to go a good ways back to catch the incredible efforts put forth by God's little country angels on this one.

Juan Contreras is about as likable a person as you could ever want to meet. The first thing that I noticed about Juan when I met him was that he never talked down to me. He listened to my songs, and he let me know his thoughts on them good or bad. Juan has been a large part of so many different artists' paths over his long career in Nashville. He has worked with some of the best publishers and producers to ever push the red button in town. We talked one day about his relationship with Don Gant, who produced the early Jimmy Buffet records and his education from being around the best in the business back then. Juan has a quality about him that seems to be a common thread with the great ones. He looks for the undiscovered talent and nurtures it to see where it will go.

While spending a few days in a Nashville hospital, he made friends with one of the male nurses there. He was a young man with a sufficient amount of hair on his head named Earl "Bud" Lee.

When I first met Bud Lee the first thing I saw and still do, is his smile. Bud doesn't write songs like so many other writers in town. He is very methodical about what he puts to pen and paper. It's as if he knows that there remains the chance that every song has the opportunity to be immortalized someday.

If you are planning on knocking a song out in the first couple hours with him, you had better plan on bringing a sack lunch.

After Juan Contreras had left the hospital, he stayed in touch with the male nurse that had a sufficient amount of hair, and I'm not kidding. Bud Lee was a developing songwriter in his off time from the hospital, and he knew that Juan was in the music business. The two discussed a possible publishing arrangement down the road.

For all of the 1990's, the favorite watering hole for songwriters and artists was the Longhorn restaurant just off Music Row. Juan and Bud Lee had established a song to song publisher/songwriter relationship. One day, Bud Lee went to Juan with a slight problem. He had been eating and drinking occasionally at the Longhorn restaurant, and they had allowed him to run a tab for his meals and drinks. The tab had gotten fairly large, and the restaurant wanted Bud to pay it off. He didn't have the money to do that, so he thought he would approach Juan about a possible advance against future income from his songs.

Garth Brooks was born in Tulsa, Oklahoma in 1962 and would move to Nashville in the late 80's. After being turned down by every record label in town, he signed a single album deal with Capitol Records. His first album would end up reaching the #2 slot on Billboard's Country Album chart and #13 on the Top 100 chart.

Shortly after finishing the album, he was approached by Bud Lee to sing a demo for him and his co-writer Dewayne Blackwell.

Garth sure enough had what would be a monster record in the works back then, but he was yet to make any of the gazillion dollars that were soon to follow. The idea of making a few bucks to sing a demo sounded like a good idea.

Now you have to see the workings of God here. It is undeniable. Garth was a new artist on a major record label. He could have easily said,

"No, I don't do that anymore," but he didn't.

Now add to that the fact that out of all the country and western singers walking up and down 17th Avenue in Nashville, Bud Lee chose Garth to sing his new song about being a "hot country mess."

When Bud Lee was trying to get an advance to pay off his bar tab at the Longhorn, he used his new song that was sung by a new artist with a record deal as collateral.

Now, as I said earlier, Juan Contreras has a great ear and knows a great song when he hears one. He wasn't just helping a friend out, he truly believed the song had merit. You have to realize though that Garth Brooks, the mega super star that ended up selling over 160 million records, didn't exist yet. Juan's thoughts were to pitch the song around to try to get it cut by one of the country acts already established on country radio.

With the success of Garth's first album, he was sitting in a very interesting position. He had signed a one album deal with Capitol and would need to renegotiate a new contract or go to another label.

He stayed with Capitol Records, but was now in a role that few seasoned artists ever get. He was trusted to find songs for his sophomore release.

Garth has always been a pretty good judge of songs as well. He ran "Friends In Low Places" by his producer, Allen Reynolds, and they agreed it should go on the next record.

It would be the first single off Garth's second album *No Fences*. The single would only take 11 weeks to reach #1 where it would stay for four weeks. The album would be certified platinum within weeks of its release and go on to sell over 17 million copies.

God has His plan, and it is unchangeable. Jeremiah 29:11 "For I know the plans that I have for you, declares the Lord..." He also will move Heaven and Earth to achieve His plans for us. He will send an established song publisher to the hospital to meet a struggling songwriter who works as a nurse there. Then he will get a new artist to sing a demo of a song about everyday people that relates to millions of people from Tulsa, Oklahoma to Birr, Ireland for years to come. Why? I think, among other things, that it is the common people and not the aristocrats that Jesus was drawn to. He could have easily been the King of Kings, but he knew it was the sick, who needed the doctor. I think it's because being a man that traveled across the desert lands of the middle east and having spent 40 days in the desert that he could relate to heading down to the Oasis himself. "Think I'll slip on down to the Oasis, cause I've got friends in low places."

She Thinks my Tractor's Sexy

She thinks my tractor's sexy,
it really turns her on...

Chapter 31

Jim Collins

Paul Overstreet

SHE THINKS MY TRACTOR'S SEXY

Nacogdoches, Texas has been a breeding ground for hard-core country music for years with an ample supply of honky tonks to perform in well within a quarter tank of gas in any Chevy Silverado. It didn't take Texas-born singer Jim Collins long to have all the beer and dance hall gigs his heart desired. Before becoming one of Nashville's banner songwriters, Jim Collins was well known in all the major dance halls in Texas. Competing with fellow soon to be country crooners Trace Adkins, Toby Keith, and up and coming country group, Lonestar, Jim held his own.

"Let us not grow weary in doing good, for at the proper time we will reap a harvest if we do not give up"
Galatians 6:9

But when you have done all that you set out to do as a club singer in Texas, the only choice you have left is to keep doing the same gigs, or roll the dice and head to Twangtown, USA.

Feeling like he was not making any forward progress, and after talking to his wife one day about the idea of trying to break into the Nashville scene, Jim's wife said that she didn't want to wait another ten years and still wish that they had attempted the move.

Jim arrived in Nashville at a great time. Country music was in full throttle. King George Strait was riding the top of the country charts as well as guys like Alan Jackson, Garth Brooks, and Clint Black.

He moved into the first apartment he found a few blocks off of Music Row. He did his homework, and he knew a few key things about the pulse of The Row. The Longhorn Restaurant on Lyle Street was only a few blocks off of 17th Avenue, and it was the mecca of songwriters and artists alike. Jim found himself sitting at the bar there quite frequently, sipping on a Coke while keeping his ears and eyes open.

One day, the Honky Tonk Angels would find their way to the same bar and intervention would open the door to a world that Jim would soon be in knee-deep.

While sitting at the bar, Jim overheard two songwriters talking about the tight spot they were in with their demo singer having to bail on their session. Taking no time to let the opportunity slip by, he told the boys that he could sing their demos for them. After convincing them that he was the guy for the job, Jim soon ended up singing his first demo in Nashville. One of those songwriters that was in a bind would turn out to be fellow Texan, Aaron Barker, "Baby Blue," "A Love Without End Amen," to name a few.

Honky Tonk Angels must like Texans because those demos would lead to more demos from yet another Texan songwriter. This one would however be the one and only, Guy Clark, the songwriter's songwriter "LA Freeway" and "Desperado's Waiting For A Train."

One day while laying down some vocals at the EMI studios where Guy tracked, veteran song plugger, Glenn Meadoworth overheard some of his efforts. He was curious if Jim had written any songs. After hearing more of Jim's vocal work and some of his own songs, Glenn went to bat and helped get Jim signed to his first publishing deal at the reigning country publisher of the year, EMI Music.

Next would come what was sure to be a huge break for Jim It was a major record deal on a fairly new country label. Tim Dubois ran Arista Records in its heyday with such acts as Brad Paisley and Brooks and Dunn. The record company was really in the hot seat in the early 90's.

Jim Collins was certain that this would lead to the fulfillment of his lifelong dream of being a country star. Sometimes Honky Tonk Angels do things that at the time don't feel very good and are all too disheartening. Jim's recording career would never really take off as he had planned, and he would soon find himself rethinking the whole move to Nashville.

After a few poorly received singles to radio, Tim Dubois decided not to renew Jim's record deal, and he was soon off the label. There is nothing like losing your record deal to make you feel unwanted in the crazy world of country music. Jim had a few months left on his writer's contract with EMI but was pretty well resigned to moving back to Texas and regaining his place in the dance hall circuit.

Enter Honky Tonk Angels in a U-haul cardboard box. While Jim was packing up his little remnant of belongings to take back to Texas, he got a call from one of his new co-writers, the veteran and later to become Hall of Fame songwriter, Craig Wiseman. Craig had heard that Jim had lost his deal and was set on moving back to Texas. He let Jim know that from a seasoned writers view, Jim was a very good songwriter, and that he wished Jim would stick it out just a little longer.

That phone call meant a lot to him, and he decided to see what the next few months would hold.

It's a good thing he did because the keepers of the keys to artist cuts were about to open a few doors for Jim Collins. Jim started getting cuts with his co-writer Craig Wiseman, including what would be one of Kenny Chesney's biggest career songs, "The Good Stuff."

This brings us to the notion that Honky Tonk Angels like tractors.

EMI had a very popular receptionist, Nancy, who always wanted to chat with the writers, and anyone else that would stop by on their way in or out of the publishing office at 35 Music Square East. One day, the wife of producer Byron Galimore, Missy Galimore, was walking out of EMI after head hunting for songs for Tim McGraw's next record. Nancy was inquisitive and wanted to know what they were looking for song-wise. Missy remarked that they were looking for another song like "Watermelon Crawl" or "Down On The Farm." Jim Collins had been working on a fun song with hitsmith Paul Overstreet but hadn't finished it yet. Not being one to let an opportunity slip by, he let Missy know that he had a song called "She Thinks My Tractor's Sexy." Missy seemed excited about the song title and said she would like a copy of it. With that ammunition, he called Paul Overstreet and let him know they needed to revisit the song that the two of them had put aside.

After getting the song to where they liked it, Jim and Paul did a demo on it, and Paul took it with him to a pitch meeting he had with the head A&R at MCA Records, Renee Bell. After striking out with songs that seemed to fit the project that Kenny Chesney was working on, Paul decided he had nothing to lose and played his new goofy song, "She Thinks My Tractor's Sexy." Ding, ding, ding, ding, ding, we have a winner! The song would go on to be Kenny Chesney's most recognizable hit and sell millions of records, which goes to prove that Honky Tonk Angels know the common people, and that there is "gold" in them little old green tractors. Once again, what at one moment seems like total failure is just God's way of lining you up for a very big life. His way, His timing.

Bernie on the set of Great Day San Antonio, summer 2016

Do You Believe Me Now?

Do you believe me now?

I told you time and time again.

My heart and soul is in your hands.

Do you believe me now?

Chapter 32

Dave Pahanish

Joe West

DO YOU BELIEVE ME NOW?

I believe that God puts people in our lives, and sometimes for a seemingly too short of time period for reasons I have yet to understand.

The songwriting community has lost some of its best writers right in the prime of their careers.

I'm guessing He has a few

Tim Johnson

"Are they not all ministering spirits, sent for to minister to them who shall be heirs of salvation?"
Hebrews 1:14

good hooks He wants to be written in heaven as well as on earth.

I don't remember the first time I met Tim Johnson, but I do know that he was always someone I looked forward to seeing. Like I mentioned earlier in the book, the Longhorn Steakhouse on Lyle Street right off Music Row was a common hang for the locals back in the 90's. I would see Tim there pretty often, usually after one of his co-writes with writers like Rory Feek or Wyn Varble.

We eventually got around to writing one. It was a song called, "How Am I Doing?" It was an intense co-write. The song makes the statement:

"Don't ask me how I am doing if you aren't prepared to hear the answer."

That's the way Tim was. I say was because we lost Tim Johnson to cancer in October of 2012.

He was like so many great writers that loved sharing his talents with up and coming writers. He never forgot how short a fall it is from the top of the ladder to the bottom.

I caught up with his amazing wife, Megan, at the world-famous Loveless Cafe for lunch one day. Actually. Megan had breakfast. It's a southern thing.

She told me that Tim had come from a poor upbringing in rural Oregon and earned a wrestling scholarship to Willamette University. He later graduated from the University of Oregon, GO DUCKS!! Megan said he loved to travel, and for a while was an English teacher in Japan where he acquired a love for sushi, but songwriting was the main thing on his radar. He was lucky enough to have met the great Mickey Newbury while in Oregon and was given the advice that if he wanted to be a songwriter, Nashville was where he needed to be. So in 1989 he drove down from Oregon with a guitar player friend in a van that had no air conditioning. You have to spend a couple days in the South in the summer to appreciate the sacrifice there.

Tim landed work at Vanderbilt University teaching English until he landed a publishing deal in 1990. His first cut came from Darryl Singletary with "I Let Her Lie," which opened a lot of new co-writing doors for him.

One day, Tim got together with fellow writers Dave Pahanish "Without You," Keith Urban and Joe West "American Ride," Toby Keith, but they didn't exactly get together in a writing room for the collaboration of a song called "Do You Believe Me Now."

Tim was on 16th Avenue when Joe West saw him, rolled down his window, and handed Tim a cassette of a song that he and Dave Pahanish were working on. Dave and Joe knew that Tim was an amazing lyricist, and figured that he would do best on his own with the little amount of song they had worked on without him.

Megan Johnson told me that Tim sat in his car at a Starbucks with his ear buds in and listened to the song until he had written all the lyrics to it.

Now I don't know how God knows what He knows, but His timing is always perfect.

Joe West and Dave Pahanish had made a full demo of the song, but it had no words to it. Not even a title. Somehow the timing was right when they saw Tim in his big Dodge Ram truck on 16th.

Joe West told me that after he had given the cassette to Tim Johnson, he didn't hear from him for a few months and figured it was one of those songs that never would be.

He got a call from Tim a couple of months later saying he had finished it. After doing a demo with a vocal on it, Joe was hoping to pitch it around and see if it had any chance of getting cut.

One day he was writing with Jimmy Wayne, and the songwriting session didn't really produce anything special (now isn't that peculiar), so Joe did what any good songwriter/song plugger would do. He asked the artist if he could play him a song. When he heard "Do You Believe Me Now," Jimmy Wayne really liked it, and wanted Joe to let him put his vocal on the track. The problem was that the record label had already tracked a new record, and it was scheduled to come out on Valory Records fairly soon. A true artist knows that sometimes to achieve greatness, you have to take chances. So Jimmy played the song for Scott Borchetta, the head of Big Machine Records, and the parent company of Valory Records. Remember what I said about the difference between singers and artists is that one sings the song while the other interprets it? Jimmy Wayne was the right voice for the song, "Do You Believe Me Now." Big Machine Records knew it the minute they heard his voice on the song.

"Do You Believe Me Now" would go on to be Jimmy Wayne's first #1 and ended up getting the Million Airplay Award.

Now back to my old friend, Tim Johnson. Such a gift to the writing world, such a loss to so many here, but I have no doubt that Heaven is a better place with him there.

I mentioned earlier in the book that I believed that Angels truly do walk the earth, and that we encounter them every day. I believe Tim Johnson was one of those angels. "Do you believe me now?"

Troubadour

Sometimes I feel like Jesse James still trying to make a name...

Chapter 33

Leslie Satcher

Monty Holmes

TROUBADOUR

Webster defines "Troubadour" as one of a class of lyric poets or poet-musicians often of knightly rank, who flourished in the south of France in the 13th century. Well heck yeah, that about sums up George Strait. Sometimes it sure seems like George Strait has been around that long with 60 #1 hits starting as far back as 1981 with his first one, "Unwound," he has proven to be a rock that just doesn't know when to roll away. Good thing for all of us.

A smart songwriter is also a smart sales person. After all, we are in the business of selling songs. Leslie Satcher is

"With the ancient is wisdom, and in length of days understanding"
Job 12:12

"savvy" to say the least. If she ever wanted to get out of the songwriting world and get into horse bartering, she would clean up. Leslie recently had a big old hit with Martina McBride, "When God Fearing Women Get the Blues," and had her Texas born and bred sights set on getting a George Strait cut before he decided to hang up his touring boots.

Leslie, a product of Paris, Texas and raised up in the world of singing her heart out for Jesus on Sunday mornings, found her way to Nashville in 1989. She would get cuts on mega stars like Pam Tillis and Patty Loveless early on. Even Willie Nelson was keen enough to record one of her songs. But for a Texas gal, George Strait was the end all, get all, ticket. She knew who to ask when looking for what Mr. Strait might want to record on his up and coming record in 2008.

She and Monty Holmes had performed together on a few occasions and like all songwriters do, had talked about getting together to write sometime.

When "Sometime" finally happened, Leslie was well prepared after finding out from Strait's producer, Tony Brown, that George wanted to make a statement about having been around for so long but still feeling like he was very much still in the game.

Monty and Leslie met at the Sony Tree songwriters' room on 17th Avenue. I love writing there. It used to be a fire station until the mid-nineties, and then Sony bought it, and turned it into a place for their writers to hang out and make hits.

Monty Holmes, who by the way is also a fellow Texan, was born in Lubbock, Texas. Both of them were well versed in the verbiage that would be needed to get George's attention.

Monty was listening to Leslie describe what Tony Brown had told her, and it was that Strait was feeling the wear and tear of all those years on the road playing music but still wanted to feel like he was young enough to matter.

Now, they could have come up with a thousand different words to describe King George, and where he was in 2008, so how the word "Troubadour" just fell out would seem to me like a gift of inspiration. It was if the angels were just hanging around the room that day waiting to whisper into Leslie's ear, and they did.

While Monty was playing the opening chords to what would become the George Strait classic, Leslie said,

"What about the word Troubadour?"

Without saying "yea" or "nay," Monty sang, "I still feel twenty-five, most of the time. I still raise a little Cain with the boys..."

Well anyone who has ever had a big old hit will tell you the deal was sealed. The rest of the song was wrapped around a powerful chorus that to this day still gives me chills when I hear it.

Leslie Satcher and Monty Holmes had their first George Strait cut, and King George had another big old hit.

So why don't a couple of Texas writers get together every third Thursday of the month and write George Strait cuts? Surely it must be that easy. Well, even if they could write a country smash sounding song, that doesn't make it a sure cut or undeniable hit. It all gets back down to God's will. His timing. And for Strait, Satcher, and Holmes, His will just fell right neatly into place.

A poet that roamed the South of France in the 13th century might not appreciate this song, but I know that God is a pretty good "Troubadour" Himself.

When You're Going Thru Hell

If you're going thru hell,
keep on going...

Chapter 34

Annie Tate

Dave Berg

WHEN YOU'RE GOING
THRU HELL

On September 7, 1940, pretty much all the songwriters I know were still in the developmental faze.

I find it extremely intriguing that anything done or said thirty years before the real beginning of Music Row would ever find a place into modern country music.... but it did. And check

Sam Tate

> "Then I looked and heard the voice of many angels, numbering thousands upon thousands, and ten thousand times ten thousand. They encircled the throne and the living creatures and the elders. In a loud voice they were saying: "Worthy is the Lamb, who was slain, to receive power and wealth and wisdom and strength and honor and glory and praise!"
> Revelation 5:11-12

this out. God knew way back then that three songwriters would sit in a songwriting room and write a song about it, and it would change lots of people's lives sixty-six years later. Man, He's good.

September 7, 1940 was the day that Adolf Hitler decided to start messing up people's lives. The Blitzkrieg of London was horrific. Bombs fell on most of the major cities in England. These were dark times for everyone living there, but tough times call for tough leaders, and Winston Churchill was no sissy. I'd take him in the third round over that little runt Adolf any day. When told that his people were going through a living hell, Churchill was asked what he thought they should do. That famous quote has been disputed over the years as to whether the Prime Minister really said it. I will tell you this - if he didn't say it, he sure as (you know what) must have thought it.

There it was, and the newspapers ran with it, and it rallied a generation of Englishmen when they needed something to rally around. "When you're going through hell, the best thing to do is keep going."

Dave Berg, Sam and Annie Tate were what we like to call on a roll in 2006. Getting multiple cuts on the Canadian smash group, Emerson Drive, including the powerfully moving single "Moments," a song about a homeless man, which explains that he hasn't always been that way. When the three of them sat down for a co-write, the expectations were fairly high, and the bar was raised.

Sam and Annie Tate, a husband and wife writing machine, felt that they were just getting started as a hit maker team. Sam remembers that after tossing some ideas around the room that day, Dave said,

"Hey, have you ever heard the saying if you're going through hell keep on going?"

Now anybody that knows Sam Tate knows that he has a library where most of us have brains. You can ask Sam about airplane glue, and he will know when it was first invented and who owns the patent on it. So asking him about a famous Winston Churchill quote was a no brainer.

"Dude, Sam always starts a sentence with Dude, Winston Churchill said that in 1940 right in the middle of the German Blitzkrieg."

"Well I think it's a cool idea for a song," said Berg.

While Annie and Dave were working on some clever lines to describe modern day hell, Sam was stewing over a different quote that he thought might slide right into old Churchill's. It's the Irish toast that my grandfather, Barney T. O'Dwyer, used to always say before taking a drink, and it ended this,

"May your glass always be full, may the roof over your head always be strong, and may you be in heaven a half hour before the devil even knows you're dead."

Well heck, if that doesn't belong in a country song, what does?

Sam reminded his wife and fellow co-writer about the clever little toast and suggested that they twist it just enough to make it fit into the chorus that Annie and Dave were whittling on.

Three lines that are pretty simple, right? What's interesting is none of them really rhymed with each other.

"If you're goin through hell, keep on going. Don't give up, if you're scared, don't show it. And you might get out before the devil even knows you're there.." Ok, goin and show it sort of rhyme, but anyway, it worked.

The song uses one of the number one rules in songwriting, Get to the hook quick then hammer it home a bunch of times so they don't forget it.

The thing that always attracted me to this song was the use of really deep, descriptive lyrics to surround the simple three-line chorus that didn't rhyme. Who comes up with lines like,

"Used the needle from your compass to sew up your broken heart" and "asked directions from a genie in a bottle of Jim Beam and she lied."

Really good stuff right there.

Sam and Annie Tate, and Dave Berg had written a fun up-tempo song. It's another good rule in songwriting. Now what? Well, they did what all great writers do after cranking one out, they go to lunch to talk about the current state of the world as we know it, and then schedule a day to demo the song.

After knocking out a basic demo, the song was pitched a few places until it ended up in front of the powers-that-be at Curb Records. Hello, I'm a Honky Tonk Angel. Did somebody say they needed a smash song for their new artist before we drop him from the roster? Curb had put out an album on Rodney Atkins that produced some success, but they don't keep the lights on at Curb with just some success.

The majority of the label felt that the song was just what they were looking for. Rodney was a real likable guy, and one of the first non-hat acts. Well, he did have a hat, but it was a baseball cap that he liked to wear backwards. It will never catch on. Yeah right!

Sam and Annie were signed to Carnival Music the home of Frank Liddell the Producer of Gary Allen, Miranda Lambert, and husband of Leanne Womack. This guy knew a hit when he heard it. When the song first got demoed, Sam Tate thought it was a pretty cool little tune but didn't quite expect the bang they got for their buck on that one.

Rodney Atkins released "When You're Going Through Hell" in 2006, and it went on to be the SESAC and ASCAP Song of the Year. It spent six weeks at #1.

I swear that people sometimes just want to hear a song with a cuss word in it, so they can sing along. But you know what? God doesn't see words the way that we do. He sees people. People, who in 1940 England, needed a rallying call. And He sees people sixty-six years later that just want to hear a song that makes them feel good about their sometimes crappy lives.

You talk about patient. Those Honky Tonk Angels had a lot of time to kill before they put that one all together, but I'm really glad they did.

Have You Forgotten

And you say we shouldn't worry
about Bin Laden.
Have you forgotten...

Chapter 35

Darryl Worley

Wyn Varble

HAVE YOU FORGOTTEN

Imet Darryl Worley like so many of today's great country artists long before the tour buses and platinum records showed up. He was signed to EMI Publishing where I wrote for ten years, eventually, we would get the chance to sit down and write a few times. Darryl is the kind of guy that if you didn't like him, you were obviously not from this planet. It would be easy for me to want to include any of his many amazing songs in this book. Not only because of the quality of the songs or his performances of them, but because of the life they all took to become songs themselves. Darryl Worley doesn't write and sing songs; he interprets life itself.

"Know ye not that so many of us as were baptized into Christ Jesus, were also baptized into His death."
Romans 6:3

Some songs truly do have a life of their own, proving once again the ever-present hand of God on the streets of Nashville. Songs can come from a real-life broken heart, a songwriters desire to explain his simple upbringing, or even a reminder that occasionally the world needs a song about going out and having a good time.

Rarely is a song created out of the elements of a disastrous time in this country. A time when the world as we know it stood still for a few hours.

A few songs rallied America after 9/11. Songs like Lee Greenwood's "God Bless The USA," and Alan Jackson's timely question, "Where Were You When The World Stopped Turning." A few years after the patriotism died down, there were less and less flag wavers out there. The nation, like a wounded bird, tried to learn to fly again with a wing that would take time to heal. It attempted to move past the shock and horror of a sucker punch that shook the foundation of the world itself.

Darryl Worley is a patriot. When the opportunity came for him to go to the fight, where young American troops were seeking out and attempting to destroy those responsible for 9/11, he jumped at the chance.

On tour in Afghanistan in 2002 with the USO and attached to a Sargent Major, Darryl not only got to perform and hang out with the troops, but he also got to go out to the forward bases and shake hands with the men and women directly on the front line in the war on terror.

When you spend time around our military men and women, you can't help but get caught up in their sense of pride and loyalty to defend this country. After leaving the troops be-hind and arriving home, he was soon made rudely aware of the fact that not all Americans agreed with the US having combat troops in a foreign country.

Darryl told me he landed in Nashville on Christmas Eve of 2002 and was making his two and a half hour drive to his home in Savannah, Tennessee. He said that he remembered on the day of 9/11 hundreds of flags were proudly displayed on nearly every front porch and lawn on that long drive down those winding country roads. Now, most of those flags were tucked away somewhere in those houses perhaps to be flown only on special days like the 4th of July or Veterans Day.

Darryl is something more than a patriot; he's country. He understands the simple man's way of life and thinking. But as a polished performer, he has to sometimes try to remain neutral when it comes to politics or religion. When he and a lifetime friend got into a discussion about the troops fighting in Afghan-istan where Darryl had just come from, he was well prepared for an open dialogue about it. That calm and fairness won't get you far with Darryl if you ever ruffle his feathers or cross a line in conversation, and he won't allow it to go by without de-bating. But when his friend was adamant about his displeasure with troops in Afghanistan, Darryl was fit to be tied. He tried reminding his friend the reason behind those troops being sent there. They were rooting out those responsible for the attacks on 9/11, and show the world that those kinds of acts of aggres-sion would not go unchallenged.

The idea of telling his friend how wrong his opinion was in an unkind way crossed his country mind, but he figured it wasn't worth losing a good friend over. Darryl had to walk away when the man suggested that America was just out look-ing for a fight.

Fortunately for Darryl and the rest of us, looking back he

had a scheduled co-write with his old pal, Wyn Varble. Now, if you go to Wikipedia and look up the term Political Incorrectness, you will find a picture of Wyn Varble. Wyn is as country as tater sticks but about as good of a songwriter as you could ever find. With hits like "I'm A Little More Country Than That," and "Waiting On A Woman," he is well respected up and down Music Row.

The two of them got together to write, and Darryl was explaining to Wyn the frustration he was feeling, and how he wanted to do a show or write something to remind folks of what had happened to America only eighteen months prior. It seemed to both of them that political amnesia had overtaken most of the country. They were talking about it, and Wyn said that sometimes he wanted to grab people and say,

"Man have you forgotten what happened?"

Fast forward a couple hours, and the song was done.

Darryl and Wyn did a simple demo of the song at fellow co-writer Brett Jones', "That's How Country Boys Roll," and were going to see how it felt after that. Darryl had a Friday night show on the Grand Ole Opry and was pretty sure he wanted to perform the song to see if it went over or not. The man that runs the Opry, Pete Fisher, asked to hear it to make sure it was fitting for his show. He liked the song. So Darryl ran through it a couple of times with his band and decided to play it that Friday night.

The response was unprecedented. The entire crowd stood up in the middle of the song and when Darryl was done singing, they gave him a very long standing ovation. Everyone was moved by it. The Grand Ole Opry show is live and recorded. People started calling in to request the song again and before anyone knew what was happening, other stations around the country started spinning the live version of the song.

Darryl said that the version that initially charted was the

"live" version from the Opry. They went in and re-recorded it with session players, and that version became the one that reached #1 in five short weeks where it stayed for seven weeks.

Had Darryl Worley not been the kind of guy that would risk his life to perform for troops in harm's way, the idea for the song would not have started rising up inside of him

Angels are very much present in wartime. They are there to protect and give comfort to those fighting for our country, and they are there to inspire those chosen few that see what others have forgotten and become a voice for a nation that was and still is trying to overcome the attacks of 9/11.

Thank God for the peace lovers, and for those that are there to keep us safe and able to have the freedom to pray to a loving God.

Waiting on
a Woman

Sitting on a bench in West Town Mall
he sat down in his overalls and asked
me, you waiting on a woman?

Chapter 36

Don Sampson

Wyn Varble

WAITING ON A WOMAN

If there is one thing that God is THE best at, it's waiting. Heck, He can wait for a few thousand years to send His Son to hang out with twelve seemingly normal guys in Jerusalem.

Me, not so much. For example, I could never run a vineyard. Waiting on the grapes to show up and then ferment just takes too much time.

If there is one thing I have learned about waiting, it's that men and woman as a rule have two different sets of timetables. For men it's, "I want a burger, I'm going to go get a burger, I got a burger."

"But you have come to Mount Zion, to the city of the living God, the heavenly Jerusalem. You have come to thousands upon thousands of angels in joyful assembly..."
Hebrews 12:22

For women it's, "I don't really need a burger, I want a burger, but if I do go to get a burger, what do I have to wear to go get the burger?"

Then comes the prep time, which can run from a simple redo of the lipstick and grab a ball cap to the full deal of wardrobe changes and complete make over— ok, maybe not quite all that, but you get the picture.

Wyn Varble is a student of life itself. Like so many other great songwriters, he studies people and finds ways to put those observations into words and music.

He explained to me one day that an old friend of his was knocking on heaven's door, and others had told him that Wyn should call him before it was too late. Wyn gave the man a call, and they caught up and discussed the tragic situation that the man was going through. Wyn knew the man's wife and asked where she was, and the man that was dying told Wyn he had sent his wife home to get some rest. He said he told her there was nothing she could do for him there at the hospital. He told his wife he would be waiting for her when she got to heaven.

Like I said, Wyn is a student of life, and those kinds of words don't go unnoticed by someone like Wyn Varble.

Wyn, Don Sampson, "Midnight In Montgomery," and Alan Jackson were meeting up to work on a song they had already started. When they got together, Wyn mentioned the idea of "Waiting On A Woman" to Don. Don had a similar story, and the idea of writing the new song verses fixing the old one was decided.

With melody and words well in place, the two seasoned writers finished the song in a short period of time.

Wyn took the song over to his publishing company wanting to see if anyone had any thoughts on it.

Chris Lacy was one of his song pluggers. She is now the head of A&R for Warner Records in Nashville. Anyone who has ever played songs for her knows that she is a pretty tough nut to crack. She is not easily impressed. When Wyn played her the song, he was expecting,

"Yeah, I like it." or "Nice song, what else you got?"

Wyn was busy looking at the new lyrics on the paper where he had written them down and wasn't watching to see what Lacy's reaction would be. When Wyn looked up, he saw tears streaming down her face. She thought the song had merit.

The song made rapid gains from there. It was pitched to Brad Paisley's Producer, who put it on hold and would eventually record it on Brad's *Time Well Wasted* cd.

Paisley really liked the song and mentioned to Wyn that he thought "Waiting On A Woman" would be a huge record for him. However, Brad had also put an amazing duet with the legendary song goddess, Dolly Parton, on the record. It was a smash single and would be the only tender song released from the cd, *Time Well Wasted*.

The writers had been told that several other artists, including George Strait, also wanted to record the song. Frustration is a common part of the songwriter's world. "Waiting On A Paycheck" could be a whole other song altogether. Paisley's *Time Well Wasted* would produce four hits besides the duet with Dolly. Records rarely have four singles let alone five, so "Waiting On A Woman" would not be a single off that record. Well heck, that's just not fair. Another thing that I've noticed is when God wants something, He will always find the way to make it happen.

"5th Gear," Paisley's next project would likewise have several hits on it, including one of my favorites, "A Letter To Me." It looked to the average betting guy that Brad was appreciative of the Varble /Sampson collaboration, "Waiting On A Woman," but nothing more would come of it from his camp.

But then there's God. Wyn Varble was informed that country artist Wade Hayes had also recorded the song and was hoping to release it to radio. When Paisley was informed of this, he asked Wyn to be patient with him because he really believed in the song and thought it still had a shot at a single.

"That's crazy," thought Varble, "How the heck is that gonna happen since Paisley had moved on to a new record and had released hit singles off it already?"

Those are what God likes to call "minor technicalities." When the time came to repress the cd *5th Gear* for more copies, Paisley and his record label did the unthinkable; they added a bonus track to the record.

"Waiting On A Woman" would be released in June of 2008 and go on to be yet another #1 hit for Brad Paisley.

The House That Built Me

I know they say you can't go home again.
I had to come back one last time...

Chapter 37

Allen Shamblin

Tom Douglas

THE HOUSE THAT BUILT ME

After 30 plus years in this town of hopes and dreams, I have discovered an unfathomable truth. The great songs were written specifically for the artist that made them great, even if the writers weren't aware of it at the time of its creation. It is the marriage of the song and the singer that makes the magic come to be.

Tony Arata's "The Dance" was destined to be a classic on Garth Brooks as was the heart-wrenching ballad of Gary Burr's "That's My Job" for Conway Twitty.

I believe that God knows that the singers will need the song long before the writer even sits down to create it.

"My fathers house has many rooms. If that were not so would I have told you that I am going there to prepare a place for you?"
John 14:2

Such is the case with the powerful and moving "House That Built Me."

I don't know very many people, young or old, that can't relate to the song, but no one could have been more closely attached to the lyrics than Miranda Lambert.

Miranda Leigh Lambert was born in Longview, Texas and raised in Lindale, Texas. Her parents were private investigators. They had fallen on hard times and had to move out of the house where they had raised their five children. The song that writers Tom Douglas, "Little Rock," and Allen Shamblin, "Don't Laugh At Me," had written would turn out to be incredibly close to the life that was Miranda Lambert's upbringing. In fact, her parents when they first heard the song, were certain that it was written by Miranda herself.

The lyrics in the song, "Brick by brick and board by board plans were drawn and concrete poured" were painfully too close to life for the Lamberts. They literally lost the house they had built themselves, expecting it to be theirs forever. The family's dog of 14 years is buried in their yard.

I mentioned earlier that God uses our misfortunes and trials to His good. He was fully aware when Rick and Beverly Lambert sadly had to let go of their dream house that a song would one day present itself to their daughter and move her to tears. It would also take her to a very large platform as an entertainer that she would not have reached without the song.

"The House That Built Me" was pitched to Miranda's boyfriend, who would later become her country superstar husband, Blake Shelton. He picked Miranda up at the airport and found her to be in a somber state of mind. She was disgruntled with her career and wanted to make a deeper statement than the rowdy hits of her previous records.

Blake suggested that they listen to some of the songs he had been sent hoping that one might be something Miranda would be interested in recording.

Allen Shamblin tells the story that Blake said they listened repeatedly to the song six times without any letting up on the tears that flowed from Miranda's eyes.

I'm guessing that Blake soon was revealed the very personal and sad story of her family's past.

In an interview with Pat Robertson and the 700 Club, Allen Shamblin tells how before his first song was ever written, he gave thanks to God for all the success that he would be given. A native Texan himself, Allen moved to Nashville from Austin and found himself working in a warehouse on the late shift.

He and I wrote one of Allen's first cuts; a song recorded by the group The Forrester Sisters. After that cut, to say that a few more cuts would show up for him, is an understatement. With hits like Randy Travis' "He Walked On Water," and the timeless Mike Reid co-write, "I Can't Make You Love Me" for Bonnie Raitt, Allen was just getting started as a soon-to-be Hall of Fame songwriter. Likewise for his co-writer, Tom Douglas, with the gritty semi-autobiographical Colin Raye hit "Little Rock," and Lady Antebellum's "I Run To You."

The two met for breakfast while performing in Utah for the Sundance Film Festival. Allen told Tom that he had been reading articles about houses and memories, and so the idea of writing a song about "houses" was tossed out by Allen. Now, who do you suppose put those articles about houses in front of Mr. Shamblin?

The songwriter mind is unlike that of any other. They store away ideas for songs for years letting them simmer so to speak until they burst forth and are fully ready to be cooked to perfection.

Perfection for Allen and Tom would come a full seven years after the song was first started.

Why? Why would two very successful and obviously busy songwriters keep hammering away at a song for seven years?

The original version, according to Tom and Allen, had more information than the final version. There were, in the first drafts, verses about rebuilding a Dodge in the garage as well as other in-depth reminders of high school memories. Tom said that the two of them kept asking themselves what was wrong with the song? It finally was decided that the song had too much information. What were the bare necessities needed in the song? After a final strip down, the edited version was demoed. It soon found its way into the hands of Warner Brothers Records head, Scott Hendricks, who was also Blake Shelton's producer.

So you tell me, what are the chances that two veteran songwriters would keep writing and rewriting a seven-year-old song until it finally felt right? How likely is it that a young girl, whose childhood home was lost due to financial hardships, would only by accident hear the song by her country artist boyfriend on a drive from the airport in Oklahoma?

That's a lot of what ifs and holy cows, but faith is one of God's greatest gifts. Allen and Tom had faith in the song and faith in God, and God had sent his angels to guide the song "home" to its rightful place—Miranda Lambert. The song would win CMA Song of the Year, and win a Grammy for Female Country Artist.

This song and this story prove beyond any doubt to me that God is patient, and seven years of rewrites prove that God is all knowing because Miranda would relate to the song when she heard it. Honky Tonk Angels know all too well that there are a lot of other people out there, who found themselves going back to their little back bedrooms where they did their homework and learned to play guitar when they first heard, "The House That Built Me."

Friday Night

I wanna be your Friday night sweet
ride summer time sunshine, barefoot
in the moonlight...

Chapter 38

Eric Paslay

Rob Crosby

FRIDAY NIGHT

I am still to this day always amazed at the combination of things that it takes to make God's handiwork fall into place. The wheel is set in motion from the day we draw our first breath. From that very second, God's angels go to work. They protect us, they direct us, and they whisper things into our hearts that we cannot take credit for. We are in the 5th grade playing little

Rose Falcon

"But no one says where is God my Maker who gives songs in the night?"
Job 35:10

league with no earthly idea of what we are going to be later in life, but He knows, and He has carefully laid the foundation for the road that will take us there.

Let me show you what I'm talking about. My pal, Rob Crosby, arrived in Nashville the same year I did, 1984. I think he beat me here by about three months. I was waiting for the snow to melt, though.

Rob and I would write with a lot of the very same people. We would both have our fair share of success and climbed the rungs up the ladder of Twangtown. But despite arriving at the same time and playing the same venues, I ended up with cuts with different co-writers that God knew I would write with from day one.

The year before Rob got to town, Eric Paslay was being born in Abilene, Texas. Two years later in New York, New York, Rose Falcon would be the bouncing new baby girl of Billy and Myla Falcon. Now here's the thing. In 1983 and 1986, the last thing that was on Rob Crosby's mind was that somewhere was a two-year-old boy from Texas and an infant from New York City that would someday greatly increase his household income.

Crazy right? Walk into a Target tomorrow and look at the first two-year-old you see and try to imagine that some day that small person would be a big part of your life. Impossible - for you and me sure, but not for God.

Through the 1980's and 1990's, Rob Crosby would impact country music with his well-polished songs.

He had hits on Lee Greenwood like "Holding A Winning Hand," and Martina McBride's "Concrete Angels" (yeah, he wrote that). Rob would also be a successful artist himself with his first album on Arista, *Solid Ground*. He would have three singles reach the top ten. "Love Will Turn Her Around," "She's A Natural," and "Still Burnin' For You" were signs of greatness from the young artist in 1991. Rob would leave Arista and sign with River North in 1995 and have marginal success as an artist.

I love that about Honky Tonk Angels. So many times what we see as a set-back, they see as moving in the right direction.

A note here. This is why I try to remind young writers and artists to always be thankful for the life that God has chosen for us, even if sometimes it feels like He has abandoned us. Because here's the thing: Had Rob become a bigger artist than he was, he would not have spent so much time writing songs and pitching them to other artists like Lee Greenwood, and Martina McBride. Rob also would have been too busy paying for the gas that goes into a road show with 12 semi trucks loaded with gear and three tour buses for himself and the crew. If that had been the case, he never would have found himself in a writing room twenty-six years after he got to town with the aforementioned youngsters, Eric Paslay and Rose Falcon.

Rob told me how the three of them sat down to write one day, and Rose said she had an idea she thought was pretty cool. She said,

"What if we wrote a song about being special to someone, not like an obligation but like, I want to be your Friday night?"

Rob said he and Eric looked at each other and said,

"Wow, yeah, let's write that."

He told me how Eric started chopping out the three chords that made up the verse and sang, "I don't wanna be your Monday morning stuck in traffic." They kicked around the idea of finding places in the verses to let it breathe a bit, but Eric liked the way it all just rolled together. Soon they had hammered out the chorus and pretty much wrapped it up.

A couple of months after they wrote it, Rob ran across his simple Garage Band demo of it and thought,

"Why haven't we demoed this in the studio? It's a hit."

Rob took a chance and sent it to Paul Worley, Lady Antebellum's producer, and Paul said that he wanted to put a hold on the song. Remember, that means they like it and are thinking about cutting it.

Worley said he thought the song was what they were looking for to wrap up the next record.

Lady Antebellum did record it, and brought it out on their *Own The Night* cd in August of 2011.

With a big cut like that, surely this would be a huge deal. Eric was already getting major singles on radio from Jake Owens "Blue Jean Saturday Night," and Love And Theft's, "Angel Eyes." Rose was getting cuts with Faith Hill and other outlets like major commercial spots. Rob sure as heck wouldn't mind another big old cut on radio either.

All they had to do was sit and wait for the royalty checks to show up in the mailbox. It would be just a matter of time before they would get the call that "Friday Night" was the next single on Lady A. As weird as it might have seemed, the call never came. Lady Antebellum would not release the song to radio and would move on to a new cd.

Well isn't that just grand? Come on God, seriously, it's not gonna be a single? Are you kidding me? That's pretty much how the three writers felt after getting such a timely and big cut. Not to have a smash single on radio didn't make much sense to them.

Again, I cannot express it enough. You can get mad, get loud, get crazy, tell Him that He's nuts, but when all that is done, thank Him because He just moved Heaven and Earth to give you something amazing. I promise.

A few months later, Eric would get a record deal on the EMI Nashville label and guess what? He knew exactly where to find his first radio friendly up-tempo summertime hit. Right in his own back pocket.

Eric Paslay released the song to country radio in 2013, and it would be a #1 hit and help him sell over 500,000 records in the process.

As unbelievable as it may have seemed way back in 1984 when Rob Crosby rolled into town from Sumter, South Carolina, he would end up writing a hit song with two people that were either still in Pull Ups or not even born yet twenty-six years later. Ain't it amazing when God does that? Sometimes I think He likes showing off a little. He should though because He's pretty darn good at it.

Django and Jimmie

Might not have been a Merle
or a Willie if not for
Django and Jimmie...

Chapter 39

Jeff Prince

Jimmy Melton

DJANGO AND JIMMIE

Jeff Prince made his move to Nashville from the sunny state of Florida in 1990. He did his homework from day one and paid his dues by playing the club scene like all the other wannabe's, might-have-beens, and future Hall of Famers. It usually takes a couple years to get your first real break in this town. It might start off as a song being put on hold, or a co-write with a writer that has already had some success. Jeff would get his fair share of so-called breaks, but the big cut that he had so longed to achieve looked like it was never to be.

"Let us not grow weary
in doing good, for at
the proper time we will
reap a harvest if we
do not give up."
Galatians 6:9

Persistence is one of the most valued traits in the music business, and Jeff despite years of not finding any really big breaks, continued to pursue his elusive dream.

If you could have picked any two country artists for Jeff to get a cut on, it would have been Merle Haggard and Willie Nelson. Jeff, from time to time, would dig into the history of both artists and study them the way a pro golfer would the course at Augusta before the Masters. He was looking for a spark, or something that would be the catalyst for them to want to cut a song he wrote. What would either Merle or Willie want to say in a song that hadn't been sung in all of their hundreds of recordings after so many years?

In the many interviews about his life, Merle Haggard repeatedly gave credit to Jimmie Rogers from the 1920's and 30's as his inspiration. Willie Nelson similarly mentioned his mentor as Django Rienhardt, the French gypsy jazz artist of the 1930's.

Now, as I have mentioned before, songwriters take words and phrases and twist them and turn them until they find something of interest to them. Django Reinhardt, Jimmie Rogers.... nope, nothing there.

Jimmie and Django.....nope, again nothing. What about Django and Jimmie? Hey, Jimmie kinda rhymes with Willie. Then Honky Tonk Angels stepped in. That's where those whispers of inspiration come from after all. "There might not have been a Merle or a Willie if not for Django and Jimmie."

This sure enough sounded like something, but the chances of writing a song to fit two country music icons, and having either one of them want to record it were unfathomable. Again,

God's timing would lend a hand, but it would not show up for a year and a half.

Jimmy Melton had been running around Nashville for a good many years when I first met him.

Melton had his first big cut with Mark Chestnutt on the tender, "She Was," a song about Jimmy's mother that went to #2 on the Billboard chart in 2002.

Melton and Prince both stay very true to the traditional side of country music. Jeff, with his love for Merle and Willie, while Jimmy Melton was the lead singer in the extremely popular local show 45 RPM, which is a monthly tribute to great songs from the 70's, 80's, and 90's that occasionally will have special guests such as Rhonda Vincent and Gene Watson. The soil was rich, and the timing would present itself when Jeff introduced Jimmy Melton to the idea for Django and Jimmie.

After writing the song and making a work tape of it, the song was played for Melonie Cannon, daughter of country music Producer Buddy Cannon. Jimmy also walked it over to Buddy Cannon. If that wasn't enough of a shot, Jeff Prince was Facebook friends with Bob Terry, father of Bobbie Terry, who would play guitar on the possible Merle and Willie session. Jeff and Jimmy received a text from Shawn Camp, "Two Pina Coladas" for Garth Brooks on the second day of the Merle and Willie tracking session. Shawn was playing guitar on the project. The text was a picture of Merle Haggard holding the lyrics to "Django and Jimmie" right before the song was recorded.

Jeff's dad had taken a young Jeff Prince to a Willie Nelson show when he was twelve years old. His mother passed away in 2003, and Jeff honestly believed that she had a big hand in making the greatest cut any country songwriter would ever want come true.

Merle Haggard and Willie Nelson wanted to record a project together for several years, but the right time and the right songs had not presented themselves until they heard "Django and Jimmie."

Jeff Prince relates the story that the "Hag" told him: Merle said,

"When I first heard the song it ripped my heart out and made me cry, and I haven't cried in 40 years."

The session players for the recording of the album were all very aware of the magnitude of what they were making. These were the last two remaining icons from an era in country music that the world would never see the likes of again.

"Django and Jimmie" entered the Billboard Country chart at the #1 spot, while hammering the big chart, the Pop 100 at the #7 position.

On April 6, 2016, the world lost one of the greatest voices in any form of music. Merle Haggard joined that already amazing band of angels in heaven. "There might not have been a Merle or a Willie if not for Django and Jimmie and Honky Tonk Angels.

Bernie with recording group Shenandoah Fiddlestrings
San Angelo Texas 2016

Angels Among Us

Oh I believe there are angels among us.
Sent down to us from somewhere up
above...

Chapter 40

Becky Hobbs

Don Goodman

ANGELS AMONG US

The mid-nineties were a time in country music when songs that touched your core were pretty abundant. Confederate Railroad's, "Jesus and Momma Always Loved Me," Joe Diffie's "Ships That Don't Come In," and Conway Twitty's "That's My Job" were just a few of the great songs coming off the pens of Nashville's finest.

When veteran tunesmiths Don Goodman, "Old Red and Dixie Road" and Oklahoma's favorite piano playing honk tonker, Becky Hobbs, "Let's Get Over Them Together," and "I Wanna Know You Before We Make Love" got together, the gloves were off, and the tender light was lit.

"In the same way, I tell you,
there is rejoicing in the
presence of the angels of God
over one sinner who repents."
Luke 15:10

Before her success as a songwriter, Becky Hobbs was beating down the highways to and from honky tonk bars with her band. One night while she was sleeping in the back of a van, a voice came to her and said, "Wake up!"

It startled her and when she woke up, she saw that they were about to be T-boned by an 18-wheeler. The driver swerved enough to avoid the full brunt of the wreck. Becky told Don Goodman that she has no doubt an angel woke her up just in time to alert the driver.

Don's son and some of his golfing buddies used to chase each other around the golf course and bump into each other with their golf carts. One day, they decided to play the game with their cars and were racing down Gallatin Road here in Nashville. The three cars were driving at a high rate of speed and tragedy eventually struck. The friends of Don Goodman's son lost their lives that day. That week a stranger called Don, and all he said was that Don would get through this and God would use this terrible accident in a good way.

There they were, two wonderfully talented songwriters getting together to try to write something worthy of the day. Becky and Don both told their individual stories and beliefs about God's angels and decided that maybe they should write about it. Once the words were spoken, the song took flight very quickly. God has a message He wants to get out. It might be a billboard, a quote in a book, or a kind word in passing, but sometimes it comes in the way of a song. I hear so many stories from seasoned writers telling me about the impact that their songs had on someone. God knows long before we even sit down to write the song where it will go, and who it will touch.

In 1993, Alabama's lead singer Randy Owens had a frightening scare. He found himself having what he thought was a heart attack. It turned out to be stress related, but it reminded him of the reality of his mortality. Shortly after that, Becky Hobbs took the new song that she and Don Goodman had written to Randy. "Angels Among Us" found a very special place in Randy's heart. It would end up on a Christmas album in 1994 and be released as a single that would initially only reach the 50's on the Billboard chart. God really doesn't care all that much about chart positions. His barometer is a tad bit bigger. He knew that the song, even in limited airplay, would reach those people that He knew were hungry for the words the song possessed.

"Angels Among Us" has had over one hundred high schools use it for the ceremony of a student killed in traffic accidents, despite the lack of lyrics in the song that mentioned those tragedies. It has also been used by the Firefighter Association of America, St. Jude, and Special Olympics.

The songs that we write so many times end up affecting people's lives in ways that we never expected the day they were written, but somehow they do. Sometimes we end up writing songs that have messages that save and mend broken lives.

I am left with the unshakable belief that in the Country Music Capitol of the World, there are indeed Honky Tonk Angels among us.

Then the LORD spoke to Job out of the storm. He said: "Who is this that obscures my plans with words without knowledge? Brace yourself like a man; I will question you, and you shall answer me. "Where were you when I laid the earth's foundation? Tell me, if you understand. Who marked off its dimensions? Surely you know! Who stretched a measuring line across it? On what were its footings set, or who laid its cornerstone, while the morning stars sang together and all the angels shouted for joy?

EPILOGUE

Honky Tonk Angels has been a process of more than thirty years of gaining access to the inner circles of Music Row royalty. With that access, I have learned to be both a better writer and a better man with a stronger belief in the existence of God's presence in Country Music. I am beyond honored and to this day still somewhat bewildered as to why I was ever allowed entry into that "holiest of holy circles."

Over the years, I have made friends with my heroes and watched my friends become house hold names. I am overwhelmed by the generous outpouring of private stories from some of the greatest artists, writers, and producers in the business, and for entrusting them to me. One of the main reasons for my pursuit of this body of works is the sad truth that too many of my great friends are leaving this world all too soon, and their stories possibly never told. To me, it is almost as big a loss as losing the great ones themselves. I set out to find the best stories that would clearly reveal God's handiwork in both the creation of the biggest songs in the country music world, but also the paths they would take to achieve greatness.

However, this book has one other main purpose. It is not a tell-all book, or a chance for me to only enlighten those unfamiliar with the stories. No, the real reason I was called to write this book was the truth, and the truth that I have come to realize is simple, yet unwavering. Without the existence of God's plan, the best songs ever written would have remained just that, great songs. There will always be an abyss of great songs lying in drawers filled with old cassettes and shelves of quarter inch reel to reels. Those great songs will continue to remain undiscovered and uncelebrated. The one and only thing that separates really great songs that never make it and those ones that do, is the uniquely perfect timing of God's grace. Without it all the connections, perfect melodies, amazing lyrics, and heavenly vocals will remain nothing more than just a really cool demo. This book is meant to make more awareness to those who are struggling with the age old question: "When will I finally get my big break?" The truth is, patience is truly a virtue. Write and continue to write. Make the best choices you can as a writer or artist but understand that your time will come when it falls into perfect alignment with God's will. Be steadfast and be more aware of those heavenly helpers that roam the streets of Nashville Tennessee looking for ways to interfere with your plans in order to incorporate His. Be patient, wait on them, and when possible, buy them a beer. Heck, it can't hurt.

Honky Tonk Angels are as real as guitar strings and long neck bottles of Budweiser with the labels peeled off. And don't forget what the Bible says...

> Do not forget to show hospitality to strangers,
> for by doing some people have shown
> hospitality to angels without even knowing it.
> Hebrews 13:2